CW00530055

TWELVE WORDS

TWELVE WORDS

Bluemoose

Copyright @ the individual authors and sculptor Linda Brogan 2023

First published in 2023 by
Bluemoose Books Ltd
25 Sackville Street
Hebden Bridge
West Yorkshire
HX7 7DJ

www.bluemoosebooks.com

All rights reserved
Unauthorised duplication contravenes existing laws

British Library Cataloguing-in-Publication data
A catalogue record for this book is available from the British Library

Paperback 978-1-915693-09-9

Printed and bound in the UK by Short Run Press

Introduction

TWELVE WORDS sculptor Linda Brogan
2007. I devised the twelve words technique in Peterborough maximum-security prison. In prisons the inmates go, 'Oh I can't pick up that pencil crayon, miss.' They've reverted back. That's when I said tell me an object you can't live without. I was facilitating with Clean Break who work in prisons. They're all middle class. Missionaries creating, 'I can't, miss.' I'm from the same background as these girls. I devised twelve words on the spot. We did it in a circle. I said the three guards, four Clean Break facilitators, and the four professional actors who had just performed my play Black Crows had to do it too. You should have seen them and the thirty inmates all hugging at the end. A different room. They all now knew these secrets about each other. Astounding. I've refined it over the years. It's dead simple. Easy. It always gets results.

Twelve Words Technique
1. Tell me an object you can't live without.
2. Twelve things you associate with that object.
3. I set an emotive title.
4. Twenty minutes to write, you must include object, and the twelve associations, under the title.

The Reno

- 1968 — 1986. The Reno was a legendary cellar club in Moss Side.
- 1971. Mosley St. The Magambo Club. Half-caste Barrie George and a bunch of his mates declare, 'No more parting for the white guys.' They walk through them. A fight breaks out. Victorious, the half-caste lads go down the Reno. It enters folklore. Half-castes from across Manchester travel there. They colonise it. **The Reno** is born.
- 1987. The old Victoria buildings above are demolished into the Reno.
- 2016. Art's Council England funded I filmed Reno regulars' memoirs.
- 2017. We excavated the Reno.
- 2019 — 2020. We exhibited our finds in the Whitworth Art Gallery.
- 2020. Towards the end I offered writing lessons. Two Reno regulars, Carmen and Catherine, and a Reno daughter, Tia, took them up.

Modified Twelve Words Technique

1. Tell me an object you can't live without.
2. Twelve associations.
3. I set an emotive title.
4. They selected an hour, the same hour, at home they could possess each week.
5. In that hour they call upon their muse to help them write.
6. In the next session we read their chapters aloud.
7. Unpacked each using play rehearsal techniques.
8. Which gave us next week's object, twelve words, title, and chapter.

Over forty weeks they wrote an intertwined memoir called TWELVE WORDS.

TWELVE WORDS author Carmen Jones
How it started. Hearing that Linda Brogan had an idea to excavate the Reno Club that had been closed for years and was underground. [Buried] Meeting in the park, which I wasn't there for. It started for me, being asked if we would be part of the memoirs, Linda was filming and getting people to talk about what the Reno meant to them.

Then when the dig started, I turned up and I was part of an amazing journey. Meeting new people and rekindling old friendships.

From the excavation on to the Whitworth Art Gallery. To exhibit the artefacts from the Reno dig.

Pen to paper. I always seemed to be taking notes in all the meetings, which I still have, I've always liked to write. Ms Brogan mentioned she was thinking of starting a writing group. Was I interested? Yes, I was. Me thinking it was a class on how to learn English, correct spelling, grammar.

Putting our thoughts and feelings on paper, going back in time to our childhood, twelve words, amazing what comes to mind where they take you, and where they bring you. The hurt. Pain. Anger. And then soul searching. The questions you ask yourself. The forgiveness.

The tears every week. The laughter. The fear of what people feel about you, the most important people who matter, your family.

TWELVE WORDS author Catherine Proctor
I learnt to write what I wanted to say and how I wanted to say it. Each week we would have a new chapter. Sit together read aloud to each other pouring our hearts out, telling our darkest moments, without judgement, sometime shock, but feeling safe and secure in our space with each other. Each week Linda would

unpick our words, she would ask questions even we had not dared to ask ourselves. We grew strong and we learnt to trust each other. Facing what had been hidden inside our soul for so long.

TWELVE WORDS author Anthea Cribbin known to us as Tia Immediately after writing TWELVE WORDS, I became a tutor at Gorse Hill Studio. Devised a play with my pupils. The biggest response I got was, 'Miss, you're writing about me.' It premiers in the Lowry. The Royal Exchange are coming to see it. I enrolled on art foundation course. Now I paint, paid, at Hip Hop gigs. Paint to commission. I designed TWELVE WORDS cover, paid. I also wrote TWELVE WORDS blurb on the back cover. Before, I was an unemployed single mum.

The Reason That I Hate

Carmen

I really don't like to use the word HATE as I think it will come back on me, as bad luck. Or on my family. I've felt hate for my mum, for what she did to me as a child and to my children, when they were growing up.

I hate being in situations where I don't have control or feel uncomfortable.

I hate remembering situations or having memories of when I was growing up. In the homes I was put in, going hungry.

I hated being cold and frightened, being in situations that I could not control because of my age.

I hated what people did to me.

I hated that I HATED, it does not make sense.

What is HATE??????

PAIN?

FEAR?

COLD?

IT'S NOT BEING YOU.

Hate is DARK, SOMETHING I'M NOT.

Hate is being angry...

The Reason I Hate Racism

Tia

From being in the womb, I've been the victim of racism. My granddad had access to me straight through the fluid that was protecting me in my mum's stomach.

'Bring that NIGGER in this house and I'LL POISON IT!'

My earliest memories of my Irish granddad; he's singing old songs, humming music from yester year and smiling and laughing and then showing me how to work the ground, observe the sky and its weather, the seasons and how to plant and grow my own food. Boredom has disappeared and a time thief has slipped in. My nana doesn't entertain me the same way, but she is the one who's always there. And my aunty, only a year older than me, who calls me the sunshine girl (but hates her big sister, my mum). I almost believe her. It is always sunny when I visit them. I know now it's probably that my mum had seasonal disorder and only ever left the horizontal position of the couch when it was sunny.

That was a long time ago. Some of that family has passed on, some of them still here but I've at times wished them not to be here. But they're still there, larger than life on social media. Wanting accessibility to everything that's going on, but I don't want them and their ignorance. Not total racists because why was I left so often with them? Alarm bells in my head. I have art now to tell a story, my story. I've done nothing but weigh up, calculate and shine a light on it all and make sense of this shitstorm I was born into.

Red Coat With Fur Collar

When I Was Little I Was Carmen

I was taken into town (Manchester City Centre) by my dad to buy a new coat. It would be my Sunday best coat, worn on SUNDAYS if we went out or on special occasions. We went to C & A stores, my dad bought me a beautiful red wool coat with a fur collar, pockets, with lovely buttons, since then I've always loved red coats. I felt very special when I wore my red coat. Posh. I remember going to the Wycliffe Cinema on Princess Rd one Sunday afternoon with what I thought were my friends, there were about six of us.

I can't remember how or why but I ended up having a fight with one of the girls at the back of the Wycliffe, she tore the collar on my beautiful red coat that my dad bought me. I lived five minutes from the Wycliffe, when I got home and my mum seen my coat and how dishevelled I looked, she dragged me back out of the house back to the Wycliffe, we met the girls who I had been to the cinema with and CB the girl who I had the fight with. My mum made me have another fight with CB for ripping my coat and then I got a few slaps off my mum.

Something I've never forgotten. These days I wear my clothes whenever not just for special occasions. I love perfume, lovely underwear. My dad always bought me the best, good shoes. At times in my life growing up with my mum, we didn't always have a lot of money, the house was always very clean, even though it could be quite cold, we used to have a tea chest in the kitchen where the coal was kept. I used to visit my dad most Sundays, have dinner, watch TV. I always got spoilt, a half crown, Roses chocolates, a beautiful cooked meal by my dad, the house always smelt of coffee. Sundays were very special, even as I got older and had my own children, we would go to dad's right up until he passed away. (Maybe not every Sunday as the kids got older.) My dad would take me home about 5:00pm. My dad's house was in Rusholme and me, and my mum lived in Moss Side. On Moss Lane near the police station, writing this piece has made me feel sad, I don't know why...

I remember my Holy Communion day, wearing my beautiful white dress and veil, my Communion was at The Holy Name Church on Oxford RD, I felt so special. My dad came to pick me up after I got back from Church, I spent the day with him at Norman Rd, my auntie Jean and uncle Chung who lived upstairs in my dad's house, they were a lovely couple and really good friends with my dad, she was very glamourous and he was handsome.

My Dog Blackie

Tia

WHEN I WAS LITTLE I WAS ... just like my mongrel dog, 'Blackie'. I'm laughing to myself as I think of all the things I loved about that dog. I think who I am now, allowing myself to be a playful pup. And I think I'm being an armchair psychologist or maybe a borderline narcissist because all of Blackie's attributes are all the good things I loved about myself as a child.

I was the observer, the quiet one who said very little but was taking it all in. I remember my best friend's mum crying because she had split with her husband and couldn't wire a plug. I was seven and took the plug from her hands, wired it, correctly may I add, and she cried some more.

'What the fuck? What's she crying for now?' I said in my head. I had a whole bank of swear words usually saved for my sister, but I had the sense to not use them in front of an adult.

Blackie was smart too; carried his own cheap dog food in his mouth while I carried my mum's cheap Kwik Save bags of shopping by the sleeves of my coat or jumper, to stop the weight of the plastic handles cutting into my fingers.

When I was little, I had the blackest, shiniest hair and my mum told me when I was born, I had hair so black it was almost blue. She also thought I was going to be born with an afro. She said I was so hairy; I was like a little monkey. She said she could call me that but not any other white person. I suppose we'd call that white-woman-with-black-kid privilege! Her loyalty in protecting my race wasn't always present, especially when she

9

repeatedly called my father a black bastard behind his back and at age two/three I repeated those words to him like a parrot. 'Black bastard, black bastard...' I wasn't born confused, but this didn't help at all.

I wasn't always happy as a kid; a serious face and got told by people I didn't like to smile more, 'You're good looking when you smile.' Code for, 'You're a little minger when you're not.' They were the words from my mum's best friend, Mad Pat. The clue is in the name and my mum had a replacement 'Mad Pat' every few years.

No one really stuck around. Not even Blackie who when my mum hit her serious bout of depression, hit the road like the Littlest Hobo.

Hand On The Step

The Reason I Love My Dad
Carmen

It's the one thing that seems to always come back to me. I remember being in the kitchen, it was a bright day, the back door was open. I'm not sure how old I was. Young. very young. I look towards the back door and on the back doorstep is a black hand. As a grown up I think it was a man's hand? It was frightening as I could only see the actual hand, no other part, such as the wrist or arm. I felt utter fear. I'm sure I wasn't alone in the house. My mum must have been around somewhere. Who was in the house? I DONT KNOW. I remember to this day how I felt, now at my age, how helpless I felt.

Was someone playing a trick??

How old was I?

Why do I remember this from so long ago? I think the house was on Kippax Street. I don't remember who lived there with me and my mum, I think it was a nice house. I ran scared, fear is awful, it follows you through life, appearing at different times and situations unexpected. WHOSE hand was it????

The reason I love my dad. Because he was my dad, handsome, kind. I thought he was amazing, special, a dapper dresser, he was always kind to me. I never saw a bad side to him. Never heard him raise his voice. But did I really know him? I never lived with him as families do, as mum, dad and child. My parents split up when I was very young. I remember the shop house on Lloyd Street. We lived there as a family for a while. My dad's BARBER SHOP was in the front room. It had green shutters on the outside of the front room windows, the kitchen was at the back of the house. My dad was a very clever man, he could put his hand to many things, electrics, building, he was a great cook. He made me feel safe, I lived with him for a short period of time in my younger years. He was a very hard-working man. I loved him with all my heart. But what I realise now is that I didn't really know him or a lot about his life as a young man or his family.

He did travel the world a few times over. I miss him. I can see his face, his smile, feel his hand on my back. As I've written these pieces, I pondered on him, on me, my life, my children, I hope they have more memories and happy thoughts of me and family history. I also realise that as a child maybe he could have done more, I'm not sure how?? Maybe have been stronger where my mum was concerned. BUT I know he loved me.

Fruit And Nut

Tia

The reason I love my dad.

Do I? Do I really? I'm forty-four and I'm struggling to separate the idea of loving 'him' as my dad or loving my dad as an idea.

I love chocolate.

I hate chocolate with nuts.

I love when someone knows I love chocolate and gives me chocolate.

I love a chocolate orange.

I hate chocolate with dried fruit.

I love chocolate, I love fruit, I love nuts.

But I hate Cadbury's Fruit & Nut.

I think I love that people who know me, know that a sure torture method to have over me, would be to hold me down and feed me dried fruit or buy me a frigging Fruit & Nut. My dad didn't know this of me. I think I almost love his audacity to not know really anything about me. He knew when my birthday was. Only because he remembered it was near to the bank holiday Monday when Moss Side used to have carnival.

I didn't see my dad often. In fact, I was lucky to see him once a year on my birthday; well, the bank holiday Monday at the end of May. I remember getting excited to see him on the run up to carnival. He'd always bring me a massive bag of sweets and a huge Fruit & Nut, about which he'd say, 'Give some to your sister.' (My sister but not his daughter.) I think I loved him for that. She hasn't EVER met her dad, though she's the most successful one of the lot of us!

I suppose it was a basic kindness to myself as a child, that I had to seek out meaning and emotion from mine and my dad's short interactions. They always took place in his big, posh car. A white BMW. I was never impressed by it (still the same about cars now), I was too busy staring at his face, wanting something from him but not having the emotional language to ask. I now know it wasn't my job to be searching for it. Love should have been my entitlement, my right, but it never came.

Our meetings always had the same ritual; 'Where's your school report?'

I'd hand it over.

He'd bypass all the A's and find a B+, 'Next time, I want to see all A's!'

I don't even know if he was joking because I do the same thing, 'jovially', with my kids now.

He'd then ask, 'Is everything ok, with everything?'

Where do I even start with that big ass, global question? Do I tell him my mum got married, my stepdad takes way too much shit from my mum, they're always arguing, my mum's a psycho and yesterday stabbed my stepdad in the big toe, and that I ran away and hid in a tractor on Rec Park?'

No, I can't tell him that and I just reply with the convincing look of a top class blagger. 'Yeah, yep, everything's good!' I'd lie.

Then he would reach for his wallet, always bulging, hand me £50 and say, 'That's for you. DON'T give it you mum!'

I made a mistake that year in 1987. I now know it wasn't my mistake. I answered him back using that big people's single mum talk. 'I don't want your money. Dad, I want your time.' No response so I carry on. 'And I AM going to give my mum this money because there are fifty-two weeks in a year so that's not even a pound a week.'

I saw the vex expression wave across his face and his chest heave up, but I wasn't scared. 'What day is it today?' I continued with my 'big mum talk'.

He kissed his teeth and said, 'Your birthday!'

I then asked him what date that was. He didn't reply.

'You don't know when it is, do you? You think my birthday is Carnival, but no one has their birthday on the same day of the week each year.'

No reply.

I didn't see him again for about three years. Could have been longer. I can't remember. By which time I was big, and he'd stopped bringing me bastard Fruit & Nut!

So, I suppose I should think about, what I do love about my dad. The fact that I have to think about it, and it can't roll off my tongue I suppose speaks volumes to some. I've had to get to know him from the little he said but the lots he did. Doing the maths and the age he was, he would have been the grandchild of a slave. Knowing that kind of makes me reflect on why he appeared to love his material possessions more and it may have been ingrained through the generations not to get too close to loved ones, because they could be taken away at any moment.

When old age did find him, and I was a parent too, he paid me one compliment. One compliment from my parent that I do cherish and love. He sat in his kitchen, the house where once he lived in with his wife and six kids and he said, 'Bwoy, yu su good wit those pickney deh. If I had my time again ... I'd do things differently.'

I can only take from that he would have loved me with his heart and not his wallet.

The Reason I Hate S.A.

Catherine

Its Sunday morning around 4:00am I've left the Reno and bought my curry patty next door, I stuffed it in my face and now wish I'd bought two but it's too late they are shut.

Walking down Princess Road, with my friend Margaret, wondering what we are going to do for the rest of the night/ morning, we can't go home our family would kill us that's for sure.

Here comes Mr S.A. looking charming and handsome as ever, he walked over to us asked what we are doing, and where am I going? In his usual cheeky way, he had obviously smoked a lot of weed that night. I tell him we are hanging out, haha, 5:00am. He invites us to his place, wow!! He is inviting me? Us? I thought he was too cool for the likes of me ... I'm still high from the music and inhaling the weed, which I didn't smoke just passively

We arrived at what could only be described as a hovel. I thought he was a King, hell no he is an old prick. He opens the door pushing me in, he then turns around, pushes my friend away and slams the door. In those days we were tough and used to being knocked about, he pushes me up the stairs. I am nervous but sort of laughing at the same time, confused by what had just happened and the fact that I was still drunk didn't help.

We get to his door and I begin to get scared I tell him I want to go home. He blocks me from going down the stairs, opens his door and pushes me into the room a bedsit: I remember shirts hanging on the dado rail all neat and ironed, there was an unpleasant smell, the ironing board was by a small window with the iron on top of it...

'Take off your clothes,' he shouts at me – I laughed still drunk from the music and alcohol of the night, his face is straight.

'I'm not kidding do it,' he says. 'Fucking do it!'

I look at him. The mood has changed, he has a whip in his hand, my heart sinks, I sober up and start crying, 'Let me go.' We didn't have mobile phones in them days, I couldn't call my Iggy friends on Facebook. I'm terrified.

He is half naked now just socks, pants and a white vest. I remember that cos I thought only old men wore them. Now I realise he is an older man just dressed in boys' clothing like a wolf, out looking for his prey. He's jumping up and down flashing the whip at me.

I won't take my clothes off. I'm begging him to let me go. Suddenly he jumps on me and starts to rip my clothes. I fight him back but he's gone crazy ... he won't listen to me, my friend has left me and now I'm alone, in the room with a stranger, he is trying to rape me, but he can't get my jeans off. We are fighting, I am shouting, no one in the house comes. They must be used to it. He kept getting off the bed jumping up and down, slightly hitting me with his whip, then trying again to get my jeans off. He finally put his hand over my mouth and pulls them off. I think I may have passed out with the exhaustion and the sheer weight of the fight, and he finally gets what he wanted.

I try to move, he won't let me; he tells me I am his prisoner, his sweaty paws on my face I am heaving, he smells of sweat and I smell of him. He falls asleep I try to move he wakes, laughs, 'You are going nowhere.' He forces his sticky self on me again, this time I lie still it will soon be over.

I wonder where Margaret went, why didn't she come back for me, did she run for the police? Or did she just roam around till she found someone she knew? That is what street kids did.

I did not shut my eyes terrified of what he will do next, daylight is coming through the cheap dirty curtain, there was a smell of must in the room. I am stiff as a board hoping he doesn't wake up wondering how I will get free; he opens his eyes tells me I can go when he is finished with me, and ties my hands together. He gets up, partially dresses himself and says If I want to go, I have to work for him I am his, and I need to earn money – he's telling me I have to be a prostitute and give him my money what the fuck ... he is punching me in my arms and body. He clearly has manhood problems, a short man, with a big ego.

He gets dressed, has ironed a shirt and putting his bling on. He is going out, all clean and smart. He tells me when he gets back I should be ready for work – I am thinking of my friend again is she in my situation? Is she safe? He undoes my hands picks up the whip he is making me jump as he hits me with it, then he suddenly drops it, opens the door slams it behind him and I am alone.

Terrified. Not wanting to move, I do not know what to do. The door is locked, I'm on the first floor, there is just one small window in the room, I wonder did I fall asleep?

I hear the door open, my mouth is dry, I'm not letting him do this again, I have run to the window which was partially open, the iron is still on the board, I turn it on. He starts laughing at me as I am half way out the window. I have picked the iron up as he comes close, he has managed to grab me, I put the iron to his face he lets me go.

I drop down on to a wall, then jump to the ground. I climb over the gate and start running for my life. It's late Sunday. I just go home; I don't tell anyone.

I still went to the Reno, I saw him many times. He never came near me again. I got to know that he did this often: bullying, raping, making women work for him, he was a pimp.

He was a short guy with a huge chip on his shoulder – no doubt a victim of his own childhood, of deprivation and abuse.

I saw him years later with grey slacks on, a dirty polo neck jumper. He looked old, tired, like an old man.

I was one of many young vulnerable girls that he preyed on. No woman should ever let that happen and not report it.

For me it was the time and era that I lived in. A white woman in a black community no one would ever listen to me.

I hear he is still around. I hope he at least feels some remorse for what he did to me and many others. I think my hate turned to pity.

A Cup Of Tea

The Reason Why I Love My Mum
Carmen

My mum always loved a cup of tea. A mug or a cup and saucer, depending where she was. What I find strange is that I don't remember how much sugar she took ... She liked going to cafés. When she lived in Whalley Range and we lived in Hulme, we would meet in Moss Side shopping precinct. Everyone knew her, she liked to pop into the little café in the inside market. We used to shop together while the kids were at school. She had a shopping trolley on wheels – we called it Nelly. She always wore her hair up in a bun and a scarf around her head, her glasses had a dark tint (I don't know why) she never looked dressed up, only at Christmas time, when she always went out of her way to look lovely. I still have her grey coin purse with her last shopping list in it.

On Mondays my mum used to come to our house for dinner. On Fridays we would take dinner to her house. She used to have treats and sweets for the kids every week. For many years we went to my dad's for Christmas day dinner, I can't remember when, but dad started asking my mum to join us. It was lovely the kids running around, dad cooking, my mum being waited on. He always cooked more than enough. She bought him a Christmas present; he bought her perfume (*Taboo*). When they were younger, he bought her *Evening in Paris.* Cup of tea after cup of tea, in a nice cup and saucer. When my dad died, I did Christmas dinner at my house. I had lovely table settings and one year my mum put gravy in a saucer and drank it. The kids thought it funny although shocked. She did it with tea; she said it cooled the tea down. She liked biscuits with her tea. She loved eating in cafés, we had done that from when I was a little girl. Most of the pictures/photos I have of her, she would be sat with a brew. Isn't it funny, I haven't got a photo/picture of her up in the house.

The reason why I love my mum. I don't know when I loved her, but I know I did. You would because she is your mum. I was scared of her temper. When I was young and even when I had my first child, I was scared of her. She was a very bitter woman, cruel with words and her hands. The times she went off, and didn't come home for days or it could have been weeks. I was neglected, in so many ways. How she didn't see it, I don't know. I remember being cold and hungry, pain, hurt, but I still loved her (I THINK).

She didn't come to my wedding. She cancelled the flowers for the church the night before the wedding. She had a beautiful outfit for the wedding. She bought me my after-wedding outfit. Why? Did she love me? I think she did in her way. We didn't speak for nearly a year before she died. When she went into hospital I went and stayed with her. Even in there she questioned me about my kids and my life. She said she had a great time when we hadn't been seeing each other. On my birthday in the year we hadn't spoken, she sent me a birthday present. I still have it. I go to the cemetery to her and my dad's graves; put flowers and cards on birthday and anniversary. I can't seem to put on cards from daughter to mum and I feel bad. I held her hand as they turned off the life support system.

Why I Love My Mum

Catherine

I am one of five siblings. We all have different dads. I once asked my mum why she had so many children to different men, she replied, 'I was looking for love'. Phew! That blows my mind even now. It is very sad and maybe a reason to love her: for her inability to be happy with herself, mum was unable to love her children and I understand why now.

When I was a young child and adolescent my mum drank vodka and smoked No.6. Later on she changed to Embassy Regal or Benson & Hedges and she would go to work in a pub.

'The Devonshire' always comes to mind. Mum would come home late with men, lots of different people, sometimes groups of people or acts who were on at the pub. They would drink, smoke, laugh, play Irish music, pop music, any kind of music. Mum always loved music. I would come downstairs and see her happy and it somehow made me feel safe, until the morning came. She would be in bed with someone. We would normally hear her shouting, 'Fucking shut up! Get to school!' She loved to swear and never got up with us.

We would go downstairs. The house would smell of cigarettes, alcohol and stale sweat, ashtrays full, maybe someone sleeping on the sofa. I hated that.

Mum had five children which she brought up on her own. Somehow we had a lot of happy times in our younger days. Mum would put on our Sunday best, pack up a bag full of sandwiches, biscuits and cordial. She would take us on two buses to Lyme Park in Disley from Chorlton-on-Medlock. Or Crowcroft Park,

Platt Fields, Heaton Park. We would go on the boat around the lake. We went to Belle Vue Circus, Belle Vue Funfair.

We were the first family on our road to have a record player. Mum gave my sister and myself two shillings to buy two records. She wanted Jim Reeves *Distant Drums* and we wanted *Yellow Submarine*. We played the four songs all night, we loved that. Soon mum would come with new albums Trini Lopez, the Singing Nuns, Shirley Bassey. On Sundays the records would go on and we danced. There are many memories like this. She took us to see *Mary Poppins*, *The Sound of Music*, all the Beatles films.

Still, she would go to work and leave us all night and sometimes the next day on our own. The eldest being nine, and the youngest just a few months.

Mum always put her search for love first. She was robbed of her house in Chorlton-on-Medlock. She thought she owned it but found out she was renting from the council at the time of compulsory purchase. That day she put her head in the oven and made us watch her. She planned to buy a lodging house in Levenshulme and now had to move to a council house in Withington. After that day mum became extremely violent towards me as I reminded her of my dad. She stopped doing anything nice with us and started going out more and more, bringing back men from the ships at Salford docks. I think they were paying her for time. She continued drinking, shouting, screaming and swearing at us. I kept running away from home – finally getting social services to put me in care. I was sad to leave my brother as he now bore the brunt of her violence, but I could not bear her to touch me.

There was a phase when she looked horrible and I remember she smelt horrible. In the daytime she would sit by the fire in her Crimplene dress, waiting for us to come home from school. She must have been depressed. We did have food but I didn't want her to touch anything of mine.

I have found many reasons to love my mum, even writing this – she clearly suffered. But I have never found a reason to like her.

Home
New Home

The Best Day Of My Life
Carmen

What is a home? Is it a house with love? Is it a safe place? Yours or someone else's? I remember lots of homes. We moved around a lot as I was growing up. Other people's homes. Houses clean, drab, cold. Warm with love and laughter. Empty, cold, sad. The homes, fed, warm, clean clothes, no love, fights, survival, being frightened of being moved to another 'home', under lock and key day and night.

Another home, far away – The Good Shepherd Convent. Nuns, habits, a dormitory home for the next three years. Again, no love, clean, food, work. Church Church Church. Fitting in. Fights, Holiday Village, life, new friends. No visitors, no mum, no dad, just letters. I liked writing letters, mainly to my mum. A visit from my social worker (once), to prepare me for going home to my mum's. A long journey or so it seemed. A maisonette in Cheetham Hill: first floor, two bedrooms, lounge, toilet/bathroom, kitchen, small, concrete. Before I knew it, moving on to a new home with foster parents after my beautiful baby was born.

HOME. Love warmth, acceptance. Foster sisters and brothers, white, black, mixed race, religion, home, church, work.

New home. With baby's dad. Top floor: hard lugging pram, child, shopping up the stairs. Two rooms, trying to make it a home, happy family. Before you know it baby number two on the way, and born, my beautiful boy. Happy, sad, out of care. A free person? Are you ever free? Life.

Another home. Whalley Range. Second floor: happy home, not a happy home, go away on holiday come back to the man has had another woman in my home, end of relationship, a very unhappy time for me once again. Happy family not working out, ask him to leave, after a lot of trouble he goes. Taking everything with him, cutting all my clothes up, leaving us with nothing. An unsettling time. As I write this story, I find myself wondering and really thinking about where I've lived until I got married and had what I call my, our, 'First Home'. I'd moved a lot of times, and yet I don't really like change. There were a couple more moves. Another beautiful baby girl. A maisonette in Hulme, our first proper home, me and my three kids. We had nothing when we moved in, but ten years we lived there.

Courted, engaged, married, parties. Love deceit cheating, another beautiful baby girl.

Another Home.

Full of love, lots of laughter, full of sadness, cheating, death, sickness, but a happy home, filled now with children, grandchildren and great grandchild. A house, home, haven, comfortable, cosy, what a home should be, never finished, a work in progress. Just the two of us now, comfortable with each other.

Trust.

Honesty.

Growing together

Not always agreeing.

Home: walking in after being away and feeling at home.

The best day of my life. That's hard as I'm sure there must be lots of 'best days'. We say I've had the best day ever on so many occasions. My engagement. He proposed in Manchester at a little bar. It was the 5th June 1976. I said yes. It was raining. We stood outside under the canopy – the bar was called *The Great American Disaster* – laughing.

The days I had my four beautiful children. The births of my grandchildren – especially the ones where I was a birthing partner.

Granddaughters: two.

Grandsons: two.

Great-granddaughter.

Overwhelming feeling of joy, gladness, love and bonding. Joy. One of the best days was watching our son graduate at university – cap and gown. One of the best days of my life. Our son the first child to graduate in the family. Wonderful pictures that capture the day.

My wedding day: dad walking me down the aisle, our girls as bridesmaid and flower girl, our son as pageboy, a great day and night partying. Still together forty-two years on.

Special Birthdays.

My 40th. My 60th. LB and the kids putting on a surprise party. LB's 40th and 60th.

Even our house parties were 'best days'.

Love family get togethers.

The Best Day Of My Life: June 21st

Tia

Is it possible to have one of the saddest days of your life on one of the happiest? I feel a bit crazy even asking it, but I know I have the date, June 21st where big things, significant things have happened to me.

When I was fourteen, I went out with a twenty-nine-year-old. Looking back, he was probably older than that but saying he was in his twenties, in his head, must have made him feel better. Back then, I don't know why I was less grossed out by a twenty-nine-year-old than a thirty-year-old, but hey.

June 21st was his birthday, and he was called Junior. We went to the cinema to watch *Look Who's Talking* and he kept going on about how beautiful Kirsty Allen was. It used to make me want to throat punch him because I was so insecure. I also thought he was a little bit bonkers but a bit of me liked that. There was a bit of an argument with him and another couple. I don't even know what it was about. He was probably idolizing Kirsty Allen too loudly. When the film was over, he grabbed a massive bucket of popcorn and threw it like confetti, everywhere! I momentarily felt like his carer as I gave a side smile and a raised eyebrow to everyone who was looking at us. The lights were on by this time too. EMBARASSING!!!!

'You, crazy bastard!' I said in my head. 'But look how fit you are!' He often asked me was I lying about my age. I was telling the truth. I was fourteen when I met him. He didn't touch me for a long time. Good of him, eh? Kept telling me we had to wait until I was sixteen. Almost honourable for a

28

nearly thirty something year-old. Cue eye roll. He waited until I turned fifteen.

I was hormonal and for want of a better expression, a bit like a bitch on heat! So, when I went swimming at Gorton Tub with school for our PE lesson, I decided that the lifeguard that I was making eyes at, would be told, if I got my chance, that I was sixteen. I wasn't waiting about.

My mind had big rooms. I was a fourteen-year-old spinning crazily around the rapids of the pool, having freedom, fun and the security of having a lifeguard there to 'save' me if I needed it. And in another room, I was the highly sexualized, big woman with wants and needs. And not far in another, tucked away, probably in the cupboard under the stairs, I was a little girl who wanted her very own man, a black man, dad, father to tell me they loved me. That little, understairs cupboard still has bits of shit piled up in it.

So, I lied. Big time. Told the new guy, John the lifeguard, when he slipped me his number, that I was sixteen. He knew I was still at school. He saw my uniform. I wasn't even bothered that I lied, even though I've always prided myself on being a reasonably good person. He said he was twenty-one and a British Taekwondo champion. The last bit was true, but you know that saying, 'black don't crack!' Well, it didn't apply to him. He looked like he'd slept with the window open and had a hard paper round. (Just to think soon we will have to explain what that job was.) Maybe that's why I didn't feel bad. I knew he was older. Two liars!! He found me out though when my friend's brother grassed me up to him. I think he only knocked it on the head because my friend's brother had probably made him feel a bit 'noncey' and quite right too now I'm old enough to see it for what it is.

In my head of rooms, I have a new view now and not just that 'mind full of space, big rooms and a messy cupboard.' My mind now has a garden where only beautiful, wholesome things live. I'm queen of finding weeds and eradicating them. So, when

I see a teenage girl behaving the way I did and a creepy guy, twice her age, I want to do more than squirt him in the eye with Round Up weed killer.

After those two older guys, I did date guys my own age, but it wasn't great. I'd made myself too old-headed and I attracted the needy, like I don't know, which was absolutely draining. I remember one guy who had not long been locked up for going AWOL from the army. He was cool to begin with but then accused me of stealing £20. If you knew me, you would know this is laughable. I think he just said it to cause an argument. I was pregnant to him, but I started bleeding that day. June 21st. I asked was he coming hospital with me and he said no and that he was going to work. He had been full on 'in love' at first and now it was slipping away, literally. I also had an interview that same day for uni but I'd decided under the circumstances I wasn't going to go. My friend came with me to the hospital where I was scanned, told I had been about seven weeks pregnant and that it had died. I cried for a minute and then just stopped.

My friend, Kerry, went back to work, and I said to her that I was going for a walk. I remember walking down Alex Road. My phone rang. I answered it. It was a tutor from Manchester Met, asking me if I didn't mind changing my interview time to later. It was weird. I said yes, I didn't mind. I don't know where my mind was. I remember my feet kept walking towards Geoffrey Manton, MMU, Oxford Road and my head was looking down at my feet and asking, 'What the fuck are you doing and where do you think you're going, crazy lady?'

I sat in the interview and Dave Hodgkinson asks me, 'So you don't have any A-levels but I've read your application and that's why you're here. But I now have to write in this box why I should let you on this programme.'

I was sat there, just miscarried and still bleeding away. I don't know where the words came from. I just began waffling on about opportunity, 'I didn't have a library near me but there was a mobile one on Thurloe Street in Rusholme and from about the age of seven, I'd been taking myself there, read everything in the children's area and when I was about ten the librarian (beautiful, kind-looking woman) said maybe I should start reading the history and criminology section and so I did. Then I started reading my sister's books when she went uni, on sociology and I found all these people were making loads of money from these 'theories', but well, we already know that stuff in Moss Side.'

I then added, 'Plus I am a single mum and within eight weeks of working in Asda, the manager wanted me to be a supervisor and a trainee manager. And I did all that without really trying so just imagine what could happen if I put my mind to something I want to do?'

He smiled and said, 'I'm expecting great things from you. You're on the course!'

I worked hard for three years and had some horrendous shit happen in between but guess what date it was that I received my degree? June 21st.

I'm glad to say I'm very cautious of who I let through my front door or into my lady garden these days and I feel much more complete than I ever did before.

That space in a girl's mind as well as the one in between her legs is a very special dwelling!

The Best Opportunity I Missed

The Best Outfit I Ever Wore
Carmen

The best opportunity or should that say opportunities I have missed were before I got married. There was the modelling – spotted when I was in the Good Shepherd Convent, at a summer fair. It didn't happen as I was in care, underage and living in the Convent. That was one. Next was working for Marks and Spencer. In those days, back in the late 60s, it was very hard to get a job with them, especially as they knew I had been in care. I had to do a medical test and an English and maths test, which I passed. Unfortunately, due to me wanting to party and go out and then getting pregnant I left. I think I would have gone far in the company. There were more opportunities, but they came after I got married and in later life. That's another story.

The best outfit I ever wore. My beautiful wedding dress. White, that's a laugh – virgin? Definitely!! Three children out of wedlock. I digress, sorry. Full-length, round neck with embellishment, edged lace, with three small lace seams fitted down to the waist, which was also panelled with the lace. The skirt fell to the floor billowing out at the back to a trail. My veil was about six feet long, edged with patterned lace, and I had a face veil. I wore pearls earrings and a three-string strand of pearls, which I still have. I lost one of the earrings on the day. Back to my outfit, I wore white lace gloves. The dress had long sleeves which you could see through and were tight at the cuff, I wore white lace-topped stockings with a blue garter. Beautiful white satin cameo knickers and matching bra edged in thick lace. My shoes were white T-bar wedges (LEATHER). I wore my hair up. The style was called a Cobble. My flowers were red roses and white carnations which trailed down.

We got married in St James' Church on Princess Road in Moss Side. The entrance was Great Western Street. A beautiful old church, gone now. I had seven bridesmaids and a pageboy. He wore a brown velvet waistcoat and trousers, white shirt, bow tie and Jesus sandals. The bridesmaids wore long white flowing dresses edged with freesia-coloured flowers on the hems and the sleeve cuffs. The maid of honour had the same dress in peach colour. They carried little posies. The wedding car was a silver-blue Ford Granada X.

The weather was bright, sunny but it was a chilly day. The church was packed from the front to the back. My dad was late picking me up and husband-to-be had to ask where I was. My dad was picking me up from my husband-to-be's mum's house, that's where I got ready. The kids on the street found a red strip of carpet and ran it from the front gate to the car. We paid for our wedding. We saved for a full year. My mother-in-law made our wedding cakes, all seven of them. We had our wedding reception at the Russell Club. My dad was really good friends with the owner Don Tony who owned the club. We had the formal reception upstairs and the party at the club downstairs. The reception went on when the club opened and we carried on back at the house on Grosvenor Road. It was some reception. I got changed into a two-piece pink velvet suit later in the evening which my mum bought me. It was beautiful. It was from a chic shop called Chloe's next to the Royal Exchange. We had a master of ceremonies. All our family and close friends, our work colleagues were there, plus a lot of Moss Side. What I can remember of it, it was a super great day, fun, happy memories, love to do it all again. White gold wedding rings, which we still wear. Laughing at some of the events of the day going into our 43rd year together.

The Best Opportunity I Missed

Tia

It's uncomfortable thinking about this; 'the best opportunity I missed'. It makes you think about all the decisions you ever made and your thought processes.

I was once an adult education teacher, working in an adult, male prison. I learned a lot in there about the non-existent level playing field of life. I noticed most of the men; the inmates; the prisoners, were dyslexic, not illiterate and it made me doubly protective of my own dyslexic child because no one in education really sets individually, tailored programs of study. It's an all in one, we'll squeeze you all into this straightjacket, that appears to have no sleeves but is really causing you to wrap your arms around your waist, pulling tight, forcing your chest out and your head up as if everything is okay because you're receiving an 'education' – your bits of paper you are working towards; a formal education which society tells you is weaponizing you into something great and making you believe that if you don't have them you've not accomplished anything.

I took the bus, the train and then the tube to get to that teaching job in HMP Liverpool. It paid well so I sucked up the extra five hours of travel and tried to indulge my kid on the weekend with material stuff to ease the guilt of leaving him with childminders that spent more time with him than me.

Day one of the job. The rules of clothing for women are pure madness. I had a smart shirt on, buttoned up, but the sleeves were three quarter length, showing my wrists – not my tits, not even my ankles but the prison education manager told me

I needed to change my 'attire' and threw me an oversized man suit jacket. I didn't even know what attire meant. At first in my head I thought he was calling me fat and was saying I was showing a tyre. I bit my tongue.

I usually wear heavy eye makeup but for the job I hadn't worn any, trying somehow to not look like I wanted to appear attractive. An older woman, conservatively dressed, but caked in makeup comments on my eyelashes. Tells me I'm gorgeous and I will have the men going wild. I am twenty-seven years of age at the time. I probably was gorgeous back then, but this woman is making me feel really uncomfortable in this staffroom. A few others begin to ask me questions. The age old one that I know every mixed heritage person on the planet has faced, 'WHAT ARE YOU?'

'Human!' I laugh. Code for, 'Here we go with the dickhead questions.'

'No, I mean where are you from?'

'Manchester,' I reply calmly.

'Don't be funny. You know what I mean.'

I do know what this prick means. I know exactly what he means but I've had a lifetime of having to teach the ignorant how to question properly, without causing offence. My back is up with this guy because I've walked in on the tail end of a conversation where he is looking at a mug that has 'Made in Britain' on it that I think has been made by the prisoners. He snorts, 'Made in Britain, my arse. Probably made by the bla...' and trails off as he sees my unfamiliar non-white face. My back is now well and truly up but it's day one of a new job in a hostile environment and my trainers are all brilliantly white and there's every chance they all think like he does. I tell him I was born in Manchester but then ask, 'Do you mean where do I get my colour from?' (That's really what you want to know, I'm screaming in my head. This is so you only slag off one particular ethnic group at a time and be sure to try and

36

not slag mine.) I tell him my mum is from Ireland and my dad is from the Caribbean.

The woman who has been banging on about how gorgeous I am, jumps all over the Caribbean heritage, 'Ooh I bet you feel dead exotic don'tcha?'

Blood is boiling. I feel like I'm cast back centuries and I'm lined up on Black Boy Lane for a creep like her to buy me. I respond with the blood boiling, masked as best as I can, 'Yes, I feel dead exotic because my mam is from Dublin!' Someone laughs. Thank fuck, I get to work closely with her. Delia.

Delia. She's a creative and a true educator. She teaches Drama, Drug and Alcohol Awareness and a Family Literacy class. She soon has me running one of her classes. I'm truly honored because she's one of those bolshy women who wouldn't trust just any idiot to take over the running of a program. She tells me that too. Tells me I'm 'switched on.' She's respected by the men and feared by the rest of the staff and probably society, haha. She's on my list of the female real-life superheroes that have helped shaped me.

My first lesson with a group of locked up, adult men. It's a disaster I think at the time. It starts off well. I make the mistake of praising someone that another inmate can't stand. Their friends start sniping at one another.

The classic 'ya mam' dissing unfolds.

My heart is in my throat. Some of the guys are trying to diffuse it, 'hold it down.'

Then it just happens. Two inmates start whacking fuck out of each other. I dive straight to the panic button to alert the guards. It really is like slow motion because I remember taking in all my peripheral landscape in case someone tries to grab me to stop me.

'Miss, DON'T, PLEASE!' someone shouts and then another and then another.

'He gets out tomorrow. They'll give him another thirty days.'
'Miss, PLEASE. I NEED to see my kids.'

He's got me right there. Any man that wants to see his kids has my full attention, but it's the first week of a new job. I'm going to get sacked if I let this slide.

'For fucksake, I'm on probation myself.' I tell them this, but they continue to plead loudly and it's doing my head in. 'Well fucking pack it in then!' Did I say that out loud? Oh Jesus, I did. They all go quiet. They don't look like prisoners, grown men; they look like kids, lost. The guy who had started it, has a massive swelling to his ankle. 'I have to report that!' Again, they plead with me not to. I snap at them and tell them to say we've been improvising, and he's fallen off the table. It was a drama lesson after all. They agree. I call the guard. He takes the lad away.

There it is day one. I've lied and made prisoners collude also. I'm shitting myself all week until I can't take it anymore and I confide in the bolshy, nice teacher. She laughs, with a roll up hanging out of her mouth. She said, 'You did the right thing. I'd have done the same.'

I think I earned some respect being my true self with the inmates but working in a prison, juggling being a single parent and travel time took its toll on me so after two years I quit and moved on to teaching in a college in Manchester.

Flash forward almost two decades and a good friend of mine pays for ten driving lessons. She tells me, 'One, it's for your birthday and two, it's long overdue. You're missing opportunities not knowing how to drive.'

The best thoughtful present I've ever had but oh, oh! Remember John the lifeguard? Well, the instructor is only his brother. He asks me a hundred and one questions about who I live with. Pure shit that has nothing to do with small talk or trying to put me at ease and make me feel relaxed. I'm on a lesson and he would be 'yush'-ing at mixed race girls down the road, making me pull over for him to have a chat. Some of them are past clients but I'm having PTSD seriously ... all I'm thinking is 'older man: young girl' and I just want to freeze or run away. I don't want to let my friend down, so I keep on. A lot of the driving goes well but each lesson fills me with absolute dread.

My missed opportunity ... not having the gall to demand I have a different instructor for fear of him pulling me up on the street and asking me why I just stopped. I'm normally so fearless but flashbacks of past exploitation make me fearful.

Even though my memories of my younger self with my Salt n Pepa head shaved hairstyle, hooped ghetto earrings, black Lycra all in one, with a studded bag and a mouthful of attitude, make me smile, they also make me sigh at what creeps I attracted.

The Best Opportunity I Missed

Catherine

It's mid-September 2015 my brother is in palliative care. I came back from Turkey two weeks ago. And I'm back in M&S with my niece Eve, my brother's daughter, looking for something to wear, as I'm going back to Turkey in two days for my friend's wedding. My heart is aching and my head is hurting – do I go or not? There in front of my eyes is a bright red or coral dress. It's like a ray of sunshine, it's half price. I look at it, walk past then go back, I pick it up from the rail and pay for it. I only own one other dress. I did not try it on.

Once home I looked at it and put it on the side and went to see my brother.

Later that evening I told my daughters what I'd done but I needed a pair of shoes and off we went to the Trafford Centre looked around, went to Next, the last shop, where I found a pair of bright red patent leather shoes. Oh my God look! This is not me, I wear jeans, trousers or joggers. Back home, daughter, me and wine. After a couple of glasses I tried the dress and shoes on and my daughter screamed, 'Oh my God mum it's perfect the best outfit you have ever bought.'

The next morning I went to see my brother before we flew. I was really upset and he begged me to go. We got on the plane. It was almost empty. We had gin and tonic and I talked about my brother, but we're also excited about the wedding. The plane lands in Turkey. We are staying at a beautiful boutique hotel. It's wine o'clock any time in Turkey.

On the morning of the wedding, out comes the spray tan, I'm standing on the balcony looking over the river in my knickers, my daughter spray tanning me. People are looking. We are laughing. Tits hanging down to my ankles. Arms stretched out wide. That done, it's time for breakfast.

Whilst we are walking back to the hotel, we discover the clocks have gone forward and it's an hour later than we thought. We quickly get showered, feeling great! Hair is very blonde, and short. Dress goes on, the red shoes on. My eyes are bluer than ever, the sun is shining, I can't stop looking at the tightly fitted dress and the red shiny shoes. I felt amazing. My daughter looked beautiful; the wedding was spectacular.

For a short time, I escape from the sadness of my brother's ill health.

Two months later my brother died. We talked about his funeral together, and what he wanted. I made sure his wishes came true, including the dress code, which was bright, colourful and happy. Out comes the dress. It's November and it's cold and wet that day, so I had a cream jacket and bought a brightly coloured scarf to go with it.

I knew my brother would love it, especially the red shoes. As we left the house, the funeral director asked if anyone wanted to walk in front of the hearse. I did, but I didn't.

I always see this as my missed opportunity to pay my last respects to him.

A year has gone by, I get the opportunity to apply for *Blind Date*. Telephone interview done. I'm off to Manchester for the casting – hey I can't believe this and out comes the red dress, the red shoes, the jacket and a scarf. A large gin and tonic at the Madison Hotel, then it is my turn: sat in front of the camera, laughing, chatting while they are filming.

I was asked what my perfect man was, would be. I said a cross between Clive James and Denzel Washington, they were a little confused. I got on great with the presenter, but it turned out I was not needy or vulnerable enough for the programme (ironic).

Maybe I should have played it down. Was that another missed opportunity? I might have met the man of my dreams, but most likely he would have been full of left-over baggage and scars from his past.

I would have had to run away. Another lesson learned: stay free Proctor!!

I plan to wear this dress on one more occasion.

Mum Didn't Come To My Wedding

Carmen

Takes me back to my childhood: young life, I've always liked the outdoors, playing on the crofts in Moss Side where I grew up. Parks. My stomping ground was Moss Side. My friends and me went to the Rec Park on Great Western Street. I remember picking caterpillars off the trees and putting them into matchboxes. I've just remembered I went to the park that used to be by the Whitworth Art Gallery, a lot. Also when we lived in Cheetham Hill I went to a school called St Andrews R.C. That's where I got into sports. First running, which I did up until 2013, when my knees became a problem, I had to have surgery. I used to do a lot of cross-country running. I was quite good – won a few competitions. There's a freedom in running/walking. You can think without interruption. In the parks there is a tranquillity. A calm. You're with people but you're not. You know I can't remember a time when my mum ever took me to a park or adventure park, to the pictures, yes.

FAST FORWARD to me as an adult. I took my kids to the park, anywhere they wanted to go, and I could afford to pay for it.

Pictures.

Picnics.

Seaside.

Any sports that they wanted to do – dance lessons, karate, basketball, running, swimming. Funny but when my mum and me were talking, she would come to anything the kids were doing and really root for them. Yet on one of the most important days of my life, she didn't, couldn't, wouldn't be part of it.

The night before my wedding she cancelled the wedding flowers for the church. She informed the minister at the church where we were to be married that she would not be there. We had people on the door just in case she came to cause trouble. She said, 'It will last six months'. We are going into our 43rd year of marriage. She had an outfit for the wedding. Thinking back, I can't remember missing her that day, that's bad. I can't remember when we started talk again, but we did. So, to think, when they said bride's family for the family photographs there was only my dad and he wasn't there he went off to the Russell Club where the reception was being held and opened the bar. We have pictures of him walking me into church. So, my photographs are me with my adopted family, the Andersons, who always looked after me when I was a child and my mum went missing. One of my bridesmaids was from the Anderson family. We are still friends to this day. That's enough about me.

The Gruffalo

Tia

'Yo Brownin, a beg ya give me a lickle minute of your time.' A fox disguised as a string vest-wearing yardie is shouting me down the street. It's not a Saturday night, so I'm not dressed up with a face full of makeup. I'm in casual clothing just trying to make it from my house on Kippax Street to the shop on Great Western Street. I ignore him. I ignore him the next day and the next. I'm not ignoring him because I think I'm 'too nice' which is what the 'Fox' says the next time I see him.

I walk to the shop with my nine-year-old son. The Fox stops me again. I try my best to not be outwardly rude because I don't want to start arguing on the street while I'm with him.

'Can I chat to ya?" The Fox asks and then says, "Hello, little man.'

My son looks up to me puzzled.

"We don't chat to strangers," I say.

'You know me man.'

My son asks, "Mum, do you know him?"

"No!" I say. "Not properly, but he speaks to a lot of young girls I do know."

With that the Fox scurries away.

I was a mentor in a high school for years and around that time of Mr. Fox, I had a year nine girl tell me that her and her friends were hanging out at Fox's house with his snake mates.

On the same street, going to the shop, I bump into an ex-boyfriend from my teens. We chat, we hug, we swap numbers. I did not know I was a little brown mouse on this occasion that had been traveling quite freely in my own area amongst the predators of foxes, snakes, and the Gruffalo. Crumbs. In fact I had no idea that this figure in my life was going to place me into his square prison of life for a very long time and have me in pieces. Not, the celebratory cake of life we all thought we may get growing up on our quest for true love.

I really have done some crazy things in the quest to make those around me be happy. Even to my own detriment.

The Gruffalo, already a difficult man, receives the heart wrenching news that his sister, his best friend, is ill in hospital, in a coma on life support. She's early thirties with a child. My heart is breaking for her, for him, and the child who it's clear is going to have the person who loves her the very most in the world taken away. The life support is turned off and I'm hurt in a selfish way, thinking about how I would feel if my sister was just taken from me.

There's something really weird about when someone dies, I've often thought. Why do the living still carry on and have sex? Is it some evolutionary thing? The continuing of the human race? And I'm pondering this question because I find myself pregnant. I know this will make the Gruffalo happy, at least, lift him from his pit of hurt.

I remember holding the pregnancy kit in my hand, inside my pocket. I want to ring and tell him but then I also want to see his face. So, I stand at the No.15 bus stop outside the White Mansions on Moss Lane East and I wait impatiently for the bus.

When I arrive at his workplace, he is doing his usual of flirting with the female customers but today it doesn't sting my heart because after I tell him this news, he probably won't look at another woman again. God, you'd swear I didn't have a degree but hey, like I've said previously, pieces of paper don't equip you for life's shitstorms. I hand him the test and his face lights up and he picks me up and squeezes me so hard. That's it, I think. I'm happy. This is so different to when I told my first kid's dad the news of my pregnancy.

So, it's my second child but it's the Gruffalo's first but you would swear it's the other way around. What would I know about raising a child successfully? Because the nine years prior were obviously pretend, a rehearsal for the Gruffalo's child.

'My child' is in the bath. He could literally spend a whole hour in there and I would let him. He'd have all his toys in there, flannels, sponges, an empty bubble bath bottle, coming up with the most imaginative stories and telling me all about them later on. We were close. We are still close. The Gruffalo did not like me being close, not even to my own child. The Gruffalo already has us both treading on eggshells. He is very disapproving of the small stuff. So small and subtle that if you question it, you are the crazy person. Like letting my son have chocolate first thing in the morning on his birthday. 'But it's his birthday. It's not his birthday every day.' I explain. I am met with a very deep inward breath, like he's holding himself, restraining himself. He was always doing just that.

My son fills his bath with more hot water and the Gruffalo and I both hear him. I hear contentment. The Gruffalo hears water, gas, money draining away. Did I mention Gruffalo doesn't live with me or pay my bills? But you would think he did. He tells me my son is being wasteful. I tell him, he is playing, washing and just being a kid. I wonder if Gruffalo has ever engaged in that sort of freedom in his upbringing but he tells me so little of it that I can only tap into the little he does. Because I don't tell my son to leave the hot water tap alone, the Gruffalo then attempts his next act of control and says, 'Well I'm not going to raise my pickney like that.'

I'm insulted instantly and hurt. I'll be honest I have often been told I have too many sensibilities. An absolute gobshite of a description for someone who dares to find courage, to sense and stand up in situations no one else will. A senior lecturer once told me that. Another senior lecturer told me, 'Don't you dare change or lose your sensibilities!'

I stare at the Gruffalo and my hand reaches for my stomach. I ask him, 'Do you mean this pickney?'

He repeats his cutting words, 'Yeah! I'm not raising my pickney the way you raise him.'

'Him' was the kid that often got free stuff from shop owners because he was told he was one of the most pleasant and well-mannered kids in the area.

I respond deadly and calmly, 'This pickney will be getting raised exactly the same way as my child in there. Your child's brother. And if you don't like it, I suggest you go now!'

And with that, off the Gruffalo fucked.

A couple of weeks later, I pass Fox and the Snakes. I've made the mistake of wearing leggings without a long top to cover my underneath and backside. I call it my mistake because apparently men are the stronger and the more intelligent of the species but have a total lack of control and restraint when in proximity to the body of a woman. I know this is pure shit, but this is just applicable to the Fox and Snake gang I'm referring to, not the whole male population. I am raising three sons today, so I know this isn't true of all men.

Fox shouts, 'Meee rrrrassss, check the size of her punarni!'

All the Snakes look straight to my groin. I feel my face go red, shame, embarrassment. No, no it's not that, it's fucking rage! I unleash, 'Is that all you fuckin' do all day, shout obscene shit at women on the street and hoard fourteen-year-old girls in your yard? Fuckin Paedo!'

He runs at me. I hold my stomach instinctively. He sees I'm pregnant, I think. Calls me a silly, fucking bitch and to watch my mouth and throws liquid in my face. My first though is, it's acid. I run off still cursing when I realize it's only water and not something more sinister that he's thrown at me. I'm vowing vengeance on him and tell him he's going to fucking die! I don't know how I'm going to do that exactly, but I know I want Fox dead. The Snakes all laugh. I want them dead too, but Fox will do.

I feel trapped and defeated, and fat and pregnant.

I ring the Gruffalo, let's call this No.1 in the handful of times I've directly needed his help. I quickly tell him what has happened and he's at my door in no time at all. We walk up and down Great Western Street looking for Fox. Eventually we find him. Gruffalo asks Fox to repeat what he has called me. Fox refuses. He isn't quite the mouthpiece he was before. Gruffalo shoves him and repeats the instruction. Fox refuses and says I was just as bad. Gruffalo snatches a bottle of water from Fox's hand and pours it over him, shaking the last bits like a Sarson's vinegar bottle before punching him in his face. Fox and his friend skulk off.

I'm back in the clutches of Gruffalo. Friends again and I'm helping him by writing a letter to Moss-Care for him to take over his late sister's house so that his niece still has some familiarity in her life. It's not long before he says why don't I move in with him. I agree. His rent is much cheaper than mine and of course I am having his baby. I give every piece of furniture, ornament, white goods away to friends and people I don't even know. The only things I take with me are my son, my clothes, some framed pictures and my cat.

'No, you can't bring the cat!' says Gruffalo.

I figure I will just keep feeding the cat and eventually the cat will just follow me as we are only moving to the opposite end of the same street. The Gruffalo gets on to my treacherous cat feeding and tells me I'm not having a cat near a baby.

I just realize the cat is not there one day.

Everyday turns into a slow dripping tap of misery. I'm constantly being the little woman, preparing his dinner, cleaning the house and then I tackle the front-room which is a complete storage room and chaos within. My son helps me. I get out his baby pictures and put them up. Trying to make the place like home for us.

Gruffalo returns from work. The same every day, goes straight to the back yard to build a spliff. I wait for him to come and inspect the rearrangement of the front room. His face drops when he sees the baby pictures of my son. 'Well, they can go for a start. He's going to have to learn he's not the baby anymore.'

I take the pictures down. My friends visit me only in the day when he is at work. They tell me I've changed, ask me where's my fire gone? Where's my fuck-you, who-are-you-talking-to stinger tongue gone? I don't know anything anymore only that the Gruffalo is taking a piece of me every day.

The day comes for my No.2, his No.1 to be born. If you've ever been through or witnessed childbirth, you know there's a moment when none of the gentle patting on the head with a damp cloth means anything but it's getting on your last nerve. I was strapped to a TENS machine which I was pressing so much I was accidently knocking it on and off. In the end I asked Gruffalo to top me up with the shocks when he could see I was in pain. He couldn't reduce the pain because I know he's not a miracle worker and so because he's not a miracle worker he gets angry and while I was in labour he storms out. I began crying when the midwife began questioning me on his behavior.

Gruffalo eventually returns. I give birth. Final stage of labour is eleven minutes which I'm absolutely buzzing over because I was in thirty-six hours slow labour with my No.1. The midwife is speaking to us both. She's been lovely. I'm only half listening. I don't even know what she says or what I have said because Gruffalo has stormed out of the room again. I ask the midwife, 'What did I say?' She replies, 'I don't know, what did I say? I don't think either of us said anything that warrants that.'

I fall deeper into a depression each day. My mum is being a total bi-polar nightmare and I don't even know if I'm responding to something chemical in my brain or situational or both. I just know that every day he is at work, I am looking for somewhere to live. I start smoking, only one fag a day, a menthol, next to the statue in Whitworth Park, blowing smoke into the wind, whilst having one-way conversations with my new baby about a passing bird or butterfly. My No.1 son spends lots of time at his dad's. I'm glad he gets to be himself for a little time.

Moving day comes. Remember I don't have much because I gave it all away but I still have a cot, my son's bed, minus a cat, oh, and the new flat screen TV. Gruffalo doesn't want to help me move the stuff because he doesn't want us to leave but he knows he can't stop me now because he's grabbed me one too many times around the throat and the last straw was when I was changing the baby's nappy on the bed, he dragged the cover off and nearly his son with it.

He asks, 'You're not taking that TV are you?'

I reply, 'Of course I am. It was child tax credits that paid for it, and I have the kids. Why should you have a TV and we don't?'

'I thought you could take the one from upstairs.'

Laughable because the one upstairs is a dinosaur, not that I'm arsed about the aesthetics of it, but I'd break my back moving it on my own.

I'm in my new place and by Christmas I've done well to get more stuff together. As I'm not a total cow, Gruffalo comes around to see his child. The day turns to night and one Bacardi turns into several and Gruffalo spends the night and injects me with my No.3. Flash forward six weeks and Gruffalo tells me, 'Do what you need to do!' I hate people who are usually so controlling and who suddenly flip the mode and put it all on you. I know what he's implying for me to do but he can come out and say it. But he won't.

He brings me my mail over, a phone bill from a phone that he bought me for my birthday when we lived together. He's brought me the wrong bill. He's brought me his bill. I can't help but have a nosy. Lots of numbers I recognize, family, his mates, some of which were our mates, work etc. But then there's this number, Fridays and Saturdays and lots of texts. I ring the number. She confidently tells me she's known him ages and they, 'Always flirt wildly'. I tell her like I often told him, that to me flirting is cheating's cousin. She agrees by saying her boyfriend is not happy either. I tell her, 'But I bet he's not pregnant though, eh?' She says she won't call him again. I tell her, 'Do what you like, I don't want him, I was just curious and just wanted the evidence of what a twat he is.'

I ring the Gruffalo at work. He laughs at me. Tells me I'm delusional and it's embarrassing for *him* that I have rang this woman. He keeps hanging up on me. I keep ringing back. In the end I jump up and down on my phone like a deranged chimpanzee to stop myself ringing him back.

Cut to giving birth. Even less attention than the last time and eager to get out of the hospital in under two hours so I can take my No.1 for his first day at high school. I would have achieved this if the doctor wasn't late getting around the wards to discharge me.

There are many more gruesome tales to follow about the Gruffalo. This is only one slice of the cake of life. But it's currently the year of COVID-19 and I await in anticipation and a touch of dread as to what that will unfold. I'll finish this another day. This week has absolutely drained me, but it's been good to put the Gruffalo down on paper. Maybe that is where he is best kept; trapped in these lines instead of in my head.

The Life I Should Have Lived

Carmen

The life I should have lived? How do we know what life we should have lived. We didn't pick our parents or where we were born. If we did, would we have chosen our parents for one? When I look, I mean really look at my life: parents, where I grew up, the shit I had to put up with, like many other kids – who would? Would I have chosen, my white mum, black dad? I don't know, but when I grew up, read books, comics, if I had had to choose it would be to be safe. Brothers and sisters maybe? I don't think I've missed having natural siblings, when I've been really close friends-forever, they are my family. LB is my bestie. She always said if she had a sister, she would want it to be me. P my sister-in-law is my sister.

I'm finding this hard to write. Maybe because what we want is honesty, a caring loving family in a warm clean home, a bedroom decorated how we want it. My first bedroom that was mine was in the convent, shared with someone else, bed, clean, a cabinet, dressing table.

Cut to Norwood Road, Stretford. Foster parents, Mr and Mrs Ashhurst. This is a family home, foster brothers and sisters, mum and dad, chaos, love, caring, sharing, understanding, church, in a wonderful house. Perfect life? NO. I was still looking for something – I don't know what?? I don't know what life I should have lived. How do we know?? Because if we knew, we wouldn't have lived the life we are living.

A fantasy life.

Money, friends, big flash house, fab car.

Who knows?

The Life I Should Have Lived

Tia

'You know that expression, 'Cut your nose off to spite your face?' I've done that so many times, just to be right, just to shield my overly developed sense of social justice. It's my strength but most definitely my weakness also. I am many people's shield, the warrior who fights fiercely for the underdog and the oppressed, when in reality I am also the underdog, the marginalized and the oppressed. It all sounds pitiful when you say it out loud. It all sounds pitiful when you simply think it because to think it means you go back in time and you feel it, right here in the present.

I am working so hard these days to be right here in the present; protect my physical and mental wellbeing. I'm looking back on stuff only to sort it all out, see it for what it is and place it in that box of other 'past stuff'. This 'stuff' has prevented my best life being lived. The missed opportunities, the drowning in misplaced loyalties, I haven't been true to me. I haven't given me my soul nourishment.

In 2014 I met a guy, a real sweet talker. I'd been single a long time simply because I'd had such bad luck at picking a good one, that it was safer to not trust my judgment. My younger sister told me, I didn't give any one a chance and didn't trust any man. This was straight after me telling her I didn't trust this guy. It was the truth. Another missed opportunity; not trusting my instincts and my developing heart and mind that had just started moving from being the flimsy material of a medical mask to a more protective shield.

I really don't want to give this man much time or much paper, and definitely not much headspace so, I will give it to you in the most concise way I can.

He was good looking for his age but constantly had to tell me that.

He wore expensive clothes and constantly had to tell me that.

He had an ex that wanted him so much she would die for him, and he constantly had to tell me that.

He had another ex, really good-looking, who now wanted him back because she saw he had a girlfriend, and he constantly had to tell me that.

He cooked well; I didn't mind telling him that.

He wasn't bad in the bedroom, my body told him that.

He was clean, germ free, and I liked that.

He had the colonial, Jamaican thinking that because he was light-skinned he was beautiful. I couldn't stand that.

He didn't like that I said I usually liked my men jet black and that dark-skinned women to me were the most attractive women on the planet. A black man, and he didn't get that.

I schooled him on stuff, made him aware of the disease of the mind, slavery had preserved through his culture. Kept it simple and gave him examples of Vybz Kartel and the bleaching of his skin. He always carried a newspaper or a magazine. He questioned lots, hungry to learn, an intelligence in itself. But my intuition was right and one day I calmly asked, 'You can't read, can you?'

He cried. Not because he was ashamed but because there was a woman from his past that knew he couldn't read and she had tormented, teased and blackmailed him over it. I helped him see what I was already impressed by; his relationship and active involvement in his kids' life, his wanting to support my kids in their lives, him having his own business and owning his own house and he had done all of that without anyone detecting he couldn't read. He had one cousin who knew, had read and responded to all his important documents, had even responded to my texts in the early days. So glad I never did get frisky too early. Sometimes me and my mouth.

I was going back to uni that year. I wanted to have a go at becoming a primary school teacher because I'd been a teaching assistant for years and I was good at it. Considering I'd taught adults in prison and mentored high school kids, it was a walk in the park switching to primary.

My phone calls from him and his turning up unannounced became more frequent. I had told him I was studying and needed a night off here and there. He took it as me pushing him away and obviously he saw it as lies. His ex, the one that would die for him, was also ringing me with her bullshit. She's a chapter on her own too but she's not getting one because I'm tired by it all, just thinking about it now. To add to the chaos that is unfolding, I receive the blow that student loans aren't going to pay my fees. It means I can't continue with the course, the course I call a walk in the park.

I'm devastated. He is devastated for me also. He offers to pay it. It's nine grand. That nose cut off face is back. That sin pride, haunting me but also that gut instinct of mine is doing overtime. I decline but he then insists on taking me out. The ex is still ringing him, and he is declining her calls. Sometimes I'm not arsed but alcohol is a disturber of the senses. I go to the bar leaving him with his declining calls and a man starts talking to me. I'm civil and then I make my way back.

He's been watching me. His face is like thunder. I'll be honest I do think, 'Ha! That'll make up for your bastard ex calling every five minutes.'

As we've come out last minute, I haven't brought a bag. I'm worried I might lose my phone, so I give it to him to hold in a secure pocket. It's an iPhone and it needs my thumbprint to unlock it, but did I tell you he was smart to have survived the years he did without knowing how to read? Up until this point I had been teaching him to read on top of my own studies, raising my own kids and taking draining calls from his ex.

He leaves me at the bar and tells me he is going toilet. He's gone for some time. I move to where I will be able to see him return from the toilets. The guy from the bar thinks I've been left alone and begins talking to me again. I'm still civil but no need to continue as he's interrupted.

'Come let's go get something to eat and go home!'

I think he is just pissed off because someone is talking to me, but I leave because I'm not really in the mood for a night out anyway.

He buys me something to eat but he says he's not hungry. He's vexed, that's why he's not eating. He's not said it, but I can see it. He says he wants to go to bed. We do. He starts sucking my neck and leaving love bites. He's never done that before. I tell him to stop because I don't want to return to my three sons looking like a whore.

He has sex with me. I would say I consented to that but not what happens halfway through. This is the bit I will make real brief.

He beats me naked.

It goes on for about an hour.

He had unlocked my phone at the club by ringing it and sliding open on the unlock.

He had seen a message from a Paul. Paul is my landlord.

He can read the name Paul, because it's very much like the name of the ex who would die for him, Paula.

He can only read some of the words in the message. His red mist has prevented him from concentrating on what the words say.

I'm begging for my life. He's so mad I think he is going to kill me.

I feel distraught I'm not going to see my kids again.

I convince him with one question and one statement. 'I have been with you every single day for the last seven months and in the early days before I knew you couldn't read, I would put what at the end of your texts?'

'Oh my God!' he says, in realization I'm telling the truth.

I continue, 'You can read numbers. Look! Look, I'm telling him I've paid £250 and I will pay the rest of my rent when my student loan comes through. Look! Look, no x's, no kisses at the end!'

The next hour he begs me not to finish with him. But it's too late. I've walked this walk before. He then won't let me go. Eventually he says if I insist on leaving, he will drive me home. I can see his peering eyes. He's going to drive us both into a wall because he knows he's lost me.

The life I should have had was probably to start with a man that would love me, be my safety, and for me to see myself content with the future. I'd dared to do that with him, before the ex, before the insecurities.

I agree to the lift home and while he is upstairs getting dressed, I jump out of the living room window in stupid heels, twist my ankle and limp away like a bad scene from a low budget horror film. I hear him frantically tear up and down, driving around the streets. I hide behind wheelie bins and suck in my breath like my life depends on it because I feel like he can hear every sound I make.

A few days later, I plaster makeup on over my bruises and attend my sister's wedding. I pretend, I pretend, I pretend everything is ok. I am then distracted by the complete abundance of happiness she has for new husband and my heart is singing and my hands are wringing that one of us at least has security and true love.

My revenge on the man who almost destroyed me?

I got him a tutor.

He begged me back for years.

He finally asked me why I had got him a tutor. Did I still love him? 'Is that why you did that for me?'

I told him, 'I want you to learn to read to realize what an ignorant man you were not to have been able to read my heart.

I also never want you to be so insecure that you put your hands on a woman like that ever again.'

The Life I Should Have Lived

Catherine

Isn't that the life I am living? Or should we talk about the fantasy in my head? Away from the chains and pains of my childhood, the memories of growing up, never meeting or knowing my father, but going to his funeral? Intruding on this person's family grief. Growing up with uncertainty instead of security. I always wanted to be part of that Mum-Dad-Children thing. Instead I had people dipping in and out of my life whilst new brothers and sisters arrived.

I wish I'd had an education; I was given the chance as I was always bright but with no encouragement, I chose to hang out on the streets drinking, running away. I only remember one person caring, but it was too late, I was a lost cause. I should have gone to university studied something in humanities. I wanted to be a war journalist, reporting news from the front-line rescuing those that couldn't be rescued, that was probably myself. I could have studied social history, walking through my forest free from the humdrum of depending on people to keep me for all my efforts in making them rich. Even when I was sick, I had to be grateful, but I plodded on.

In my world I would live in the country walk through the forest with my three daughters laughing, home schooling, free from the bureaucracy, away from the yes sir no sir, we would walk for miles my daughters and me with dad telling them stories of how he 'went to sea and saved the world'. In reality he was sat in the pub, drunk coming home late more beer cigarette smoke everywhere, nasty comments, a broken nose ... this was not how it was meant to be.

My life should have been filled with kindness, caring, sharing. A life where I worked for me and my family and helping those that needed help. The poor children – abused and scared, frightened to say anything, I wanted to be their saviour. Instead I had to save myself, rescue my children, keep them safe the best way I could. I wanted to be creative, show everyone how to be self-aware, teach my girls to be strong, walk with their heads held high, be proud of who they are, love themselves, love myself ... Instead, I went to dark places where I listened to the music, came out late, was abused and mistreated, but I went back time and time again. I think I felt safe with the music.

I wanted to look after Douglas, keep him safe away from danger – but he died. I drank wine and cried.

I'm not sure about the life I should have lived – working from home, living with a lifelong partner, a house in the country – I am a free spirit, always have been, and I am thankful for the life I have lived with so many layers, colourful, dark, happy, sad, never interested in material things. Catherine Proctor is a happy person. Without my life I would not be sitting here today writing this for the Reno memoirs.

The life I should have lived stays in my head for rainy days.

Convent Of The Good Shepherd
Staplehurst Kent

Carmen

I have to tell you of the journey of getting to the Convent, I was thirteen, I went from Manchester Piccadilly train station to London Euston, then on another train to Staplehurst Kent. Travelling with a probation officer, I can't remember her name, it seemed like a very long journey, she bought me treats, I remember arriving at the convent, it was a bright and sunny day, all greenery, a long drive to walk up (all gravel) as I try and remember who greeted us and what door we went through, I can't. Mother Superior was called Mother Consolata, tiny, petite, with a very round face. Small elegant hands, a kindly face, she was to turn out to be a very strong firm woman. The convent had four houses which we girls lived in. They were on the first floor, polished floors, each dorm had a sitting room, quite large with old fashioned furniture, a large rug small reading chairs and card table. You then went through another door which led you to the dorm where we slept, it was partitioned off into rooms which the girls shared, normally two or four. We had a bedside cabinet, bed and a chair with one small dressing table. It was like a prefab – paper-thin walls. A very small corridor at the bottom was our House Mother's cell where she slept.

Our day started very early, probably about seven o'clock – wash and dress, go downstairs for breakfast, which we served ourselves. Long tables. Each house had their own table.

We would assemble in the big hall, which was our recreation room. There was a TV, a podium where the sisters sat and watched us, it had lots of old-fashioned sash windows, doors at both ends of the room. One of the doors opened onto a patio and garden area. There was a bungalow near the patio area with a small swimming pool, it was for the girls who were getting ready to leave the convent, more about that later. The nuns were called 'Mother'. We had Mother Consolata she was the head Boss. Mother Joan she was very stern, tall, slim and wore glasses. Mother Teddy Bear, older, jolly, chubby, caring. Mother Magdalena. Mother Delores. Mother Bennet. Mother Angela. Mother Bernard. They moved with an ease, swiftly and very quietly. We had daily tasks, chores, jobs to do. Each day of the week, different day for different jobs. Monday and Tuesday were laundry days. Where we had to wash, dry and press the nuns' habits and all the bedding for the girls and nuns. The laundry from the manor house. That was a hard job, massive presses, big washing machines all metal, big linen baskets that we had to empty, the heat was unbearable, the floors slippery, child labour for nothing. We got a weekly allowance so we could buy our necessities and treats and stamps from the tuck shop. I digress. Back to our jobs. One was in the factory, it was assembling red plastic chocolate dispensers like tills, you filled them with mini-Cadbury square chocolates, you would pull a little drawer out and a chocolate would pop out. I remember pinching the chocolate when we got a chance. Then there was the kitchen duty, peeling the potatoes, onions, clearing the tables and washing the big pots. We had lessons in English, maths, religious studies. Small groups, old school desks. Sewing classes. I enjoyed them. We sewed, knitted and crocheted. We used to go over to the manor house for these lessons, there were ladies who I now believe lived there in the manor house, there was one in particular who smelt of cigarette smoke and had really long nails she always dressed nice.

Every evening after our meal, we would have free time in the rec room. Watch TV. I'm sure it was a limited time. We went to Church a lot. Benediction, Confession, Mass. There was only myself and another girl from Manchester at the convent. The other girls were from London areas around Kent. The girls were in groups, the black girls, the Hispanic girls, the biker girls. There were fights among the groups. Who was top dog? It was the first time in my life that I never ran away, I think it was too far. At the end of rec time, we used to line up in single file, then Mother Consolata or Mother Joan would hand out our meds. I know I got meds, but I don't remember what for.

I remember Mother Consolata arranged for some of us to go on a trip to France. I'd never had a passport, so we had to have our pictures taken, I remember having my hair and makeup done, I did them. Do you remember metal pins? When you take the pins out you look like you've had a curly perm. I did my makeup like Twiggy. I had lashes drawn on my lower lashes, and false lashes on top lashes. I wore a light blue crocheted jumper, I thought I looked fabulous, I'm sure I have that picture somewhere. My first ever trip abroad. To Boulogne France. We travelled on a big ship, very grand. We visited a fair. When we arrived back home the girl I shared the dorm with had taken an overdose, when I checked my stash of pills, some had gone missing. When she came back into the dorm, we had a major fight. From that day until we went into the bungalow, we never spoke to each other again.

We were in the Chalet (bungalow) together. The Chalet was where a group of us lived together, getting ready (preparing) to join the outside world, learning how to take care of ourselves, cooking cleaning shopping, the value of money. We were allowed to go into the village on a Saturday, we had a teacher who lived in the village she was Welsh and very nice. We had prefects who accompanied us, it was great at first but then yeah someone started stealing stuff, and the shopkeepers complained. We were on lockdown, all privileges stopped. That in turn made all the girls go mad, fights broke out, tempers flared up. There was unrest between some of the girls, I remember one girl got burned with a straightening iron, someone else had her head busted. They brought in the big chiefs, board of governors and the Bishop.

First Love 1988-1991

Tia

'Fit Bit!' The first word I ever said to him, well, the first word I ever shouted whilst balancing stood up on a piece of playground equipment, well too small for my teenage body. He looked, smiled and put his head down. If he wasn't black, I'd swear he was blushing.

My friend Melanie had told me to say it. She had spent the best part of the day from late morning doing the equivalent of a bum-showing builder – wolf whistling at anything male that had passed with a pulse. She only quit it when they were 'granddad' age. Looking back, they were probably not old enough to be her dad, but she had standards in her own head.

I had standards too up until that moment, refused her 'command' of instructing me to catcall, wolf whistle, and fit bit chant all the rest of the guys that had passed, but him, I didn't need telling twice.

'Fit Bit!' I hear my voice echo back in my head followed by the thought, 'Why have you done that, knob head?'

His eyes were kind, and his looks were bashful, and he was sooooooo tall! I must say I've struggled to ever find a boyfriend that tall since. And so, he was affectionately known by his friends as Legs, short for his nickname Crazy Legs Crane. But 'Legs' for short because who could say all that with a fruit pastel or a toffo in your gob. His mum Carol Atta would be on board calling him Legs also, in time.

The first day I ever saw Danny, on a Saturday, was one of my fondest memories. My mum, who had been a carefree, single parent all my life was now playing at the respectful married wife to my 'new' stepdad and was being a complete nightmare in the process. So when my best friend from my old street had called the house phone and asked me was I playing out (yes, thirteen-year-olds used to play out) I jumped at the chance to escape the unfolding drama in my house. I had learned to read my mum's signs and the one before a total schitz out was the unresponsive silence.

'Mum can I go out?'

No answer so I pretend she has replied, 'With who?'

'I'm going out with Melanie.'

Still no response. I'll pretend she asked, ''Til when?'

'She's never allowed out long, so I'll be home in about three hours.'

No response again. I'll pretend she said ok. I just tell her and my stepdad I'm off out and give up on the asking. I'd been a good kid up until then. I sounded so cheeky and I was often rude to my stepdad when I look back. The poor man was....is a good man, but no fucks given back then. I used to think his thick western African accent was telling me off every time he spoke to me and for that reason, I thought he was a total prick. Plus, that and I heard him and my mum slag off West Indian people and since I was the only offspring in the family from Caribbean descent I felt a bit victimized.

So, off I went to join my mate Melanie to prowl and wolf whistle boys, well watch her do it. She hadn't whistled Danny. She used to say, and I'm laughing now but I seriously eye rolled her back then, 'Nar, he's black. You have 'im, I only like the white and 'arfcast ones!'

I'd quietly grumble through gritted teeth, 'Stop saying that WORD. GOD. Fuckinel, you don't even give us the whole word half. What's arf?' I said sounding like a wounded sea lion explaining.

'Mixed-race, then. Gawd!' She said reluctantly and then would do a massive inhale that would instantly inflate her chest and then she would breathe out hard through the side of her mouth which would flick her fringe up. This was her defensive and deep down, bemoaning habit.

Danny came over to us on the little play-park at the back of the brewery estate on Denmark Road. To me lads weren't usually that confident on their own. He chatted for a while until Melanie said,

'She fancies you. Do you fancy her?'

Ground crack open, let me fall in and swallow me whole. This girl had no filter. Literally no filter. Remind me to tell you how she almost caused our science teacher to have a nervous breakdown, which resulted in me assaulting her over the gas taps. We had lots of fights. The only girl I fought with and five minutes later we'd be friends again. But it's just dawned on me, she was an only child, so I was probably in fact like a sibling to her. Like a pair of pups, ear biting was substituted for insults and hair pulling.

So, Danny is posed with the question. I am still waiting for the ground to do its stuff and Melanie is grinning ear to ear and turning her head to him then me and back to him. We both eventually lock eyes and we both instantly look away and try not to grin.

Melanie breaks the silence and bawls out, 'Give her your number then and tell her where you live.' I think Melanie was the up and coming, soon to be recognized ADHD crew. It wasn't a thing back then. She always had a fizzy can of pop in her hand, while I thought I was healthier drinking a lucozade because that's what you'd get when you were ill so we figured it was like medicine.

Danny explains to me that his mum would probably grill us if he gave us his house number and we were to mess about on the phone. Which ringing boys up from stinking phone boxes where tramps and drunks harboured, was a thing back then. Straight away my mind acknowledges he has a strict mum so we, well 'I', don't get his number but he asks where I live, and it turns out that only Crofton Street divides us. He's on Leslie Street and I'm on Rita Avenue. Quick thinking, Mel says, 'Oh we live that way!'

Danny says he has to go, says bye and then Melanie 'tells' me we are following him. This is what stalking looked like back in the day but then it was called being a clingon and I suppose we were a pair of little shits to some. But Danny is not looking at us like we're clingons so it's just smiles all around.

As we get closer to our own streets, Melanie pipes up, 'I think you two should have a snog and see if you like each other.' My stomach turns with complete absolute fear and excitement. A feeling we try to find and relive when we're older but with maturity we realize we don't want the feeling of fear in the pit of our stomachs.

I'd never kissed a boy before. Well, I'd had someone kiss me, but I was ill prepared and never saw it coming. Being on four wheeled roller skates meant I had lost balance and head butted him on the chin. Ten-year-old, taken advantage of girl, nearly knocks out fifteen-year-old boy. After trying to snog my face off, he was mortified, or pretended to be (insert eye roll) when I told him my age. Although looking at my ten-year-old self in pictures, I look like I was married with a couple of kids. However, I was his sister's age, so he was just a horny teen.

Back to Danny. The idea of snogging someone I actually wanted to, was an indescribable feeling but a good one, once I'd pushed down the fear. I had to tip toe and he had to A-line his legs and crick his neck to make himself a little shorter and go in for the first kiss of the year, up a wall in an alley. Classy.

We were inseparable after that. You could say on any given sunny day we'd be on the grass in the gardens of Platt Hall and on rainy days it was either the bowling dome or pinning each other to the walls of Witches' Tunnel. Nearer to home it was huddling in the doorway of the factory steps next to Rusholme Bumpy Slide Play-park. We were in each other's pockets so much that his strict mum decided I was a nice girl and allowed me and

Danny the privacy of the back room but Mitzy the dog had to keep us separated in case of any spoon action. His brother hated me, but I think he just hated himself. My mum hated all boys, but she tried a different tactic with Danny and tried to knock me off him by giving him the shopping trolley and sending him to Kwik Save. I wanted to die of embarrassment. There wasn't a young black lad alive in my world that would pull a shopping trolley. All street cred would be gone. My mum was banking on this. In my head I thought, 'You bitch! And what a clever way to break someone up.'

Danny took the shopping list, the money and the shopping trolley and went to Kwik Save. Came back with the stuff and we stayed solid for another three years. I think my mum knew me better than I knew myself. She was good at reading people. I think she knew Danny was a bit of a chameleon. For example, he went to London for two weeks, came back and was talking cockney. He did it all week. It irritated the absolute hell out of me. Everyone went along with his new way of talking without question. I finished with him after shouting at him in front of everyone that if he'd have gone to Pakistan for two weeks, he wouldn't have come back talking any different?

Although we had been both loved up, we both had been proper little knobheads; him for his amateur dramatics and me for my schitzo impatience and temper. Well I was learning first-hand from my mother. I'd finish with him on average once a fortnight over silly things. Because we shared the same friends, I think I was looked on as the insensitive one after I would pay Danny no mind after he'd punched the metal factory gate one too many times. He'd then wail like a wounded animal. Our friends would say, 'Don't be sly.' And then we'd be back on again. This was happening more and more. He moved on from punching the gates to faking asthma attacks. I had enough one day and asked his mum. She said he'd not had asthma for years. I proved his fake asthma midflow through an episode by saying, 'Ok, ok, I'll go back out with you.' He immediately stopped hyperventilating. I then said to everyone, 'I told you he was faking!'

He told me years later he was having panic attacks. I'm such a little bitch but I was fifteen and didn't know about that sort of stuff. That boy went through a lot of chaos back then. After going our separate ways and having our own families, we got back in touch when my mum died. He helped me a lot. I then helped him through a really tough time too.

Danny is one of my best friends from childhood and he is still considered a good lock heart friend now. He's my safe space and I'm his when we need it, which I'm glad to say isn't that often now we live calmer lives. But I am glad I have had and have his love in my life, which in turn makes him a love of my life.

When I Was A Financial Advisor

Catherine

It is the summer of 1999, Mr Proctor and I have broken up for about two years now and it's time for me to look for a house, the martial home has been sold – he kindly kept all the money. But somehow sneaked back into our lives after not hearing from him for two years or receiving a penny from him for the children. (He kept to his promise.) As usual he was feeling sorry for himself as one of his friends had died. He asked to see the girls I asked them if they wanted to meet him and they said yes. After a couple of days of him being around not staying at my house I might add, he told the girls and myself he would give me the deposit to buy another house as we were living in private rented at the time. I though I'd better act quickly so I found a house made an offer which was accepted, then arranged to see the mortgage consultant at Bridgford's in Marple. On the day of our meeting she was off sick. As they could not get in touch with me the area manager took her place. A cute polite little man by the name of Simon who fondly became known as Spud-head due to the size and shape of his head. We went through the information he required with Mr Proctor sitting there listening (Proctor was not aware that I was a Liquid Petroleum Gas rep and earned money). The arrangement we had was that he would pay the deposit and I would pay the mortgage. Application submitted Proctor and I go our separate ways.

Simon contacted me to go through some legal points on the mortgage application. Whilst I was with him, he said I should come and work for them. I was a little taken aback and shrugged it off, later that week he called me whilst with the director of the company and asked if they could come and see me. I saw no reason to say no apart from the fact all three girls were running wild, when they arrived they were greeted by three gymnasts – well that's how the girls saw themselves, they were wild. Each one showing off more than the other until one of them started brushing Simon (director's) hair. I decided to draw a line on the meeting at that point. Some weeks later when Proctor had done a runner without paying the promised deposit and letting his children down again I had to drop out of the purchase. Simon called and invited me for a formal interview and I was in. Eventually passed all my exams and I became a qualified IFA.

This was a very social period of my life always being invited to lenders' dinners, solicitor lunches, client celebrations.

On October 31st we'd all been out for a corporate dinner with a lender who was hoping to get our business, ending up partying at Simon the director's house in the Cheshire countryside, when I received a phone call from the babysitter's mum saying she had to come home, she was supposed to be staying overnight. I tried to get a cab but there wasn't one as it was the early hours of the morning by this time. Eventually Simon gave me the keys to his two-day-old five series BMW, OMG!!! We were both so drunk.

I got in the car and drove out of the driveway, that's all I remember until I woke up.

I could hear a strange whirring noise. Not too sure what it was, I opened the car door and I find the front of the car was a few feet off the ground. I jumped out and I can see the car is a complete V shape, I thought I had hit a tree, however it was a telegraph pole which was lying across the road. This connected most of the house alarms in the area to the local police station. I could also see the farmer's fence had got in the way. I'm not sure what to do, so I walk away from the car, and come across a phone box, where I try to call Simon. There's no reply. I find out later that he was found asleep on his driveway. Leaving the call box, a mini pulls up. They ask me if the car is mine. I say no. They told me they have called the police, I tell them to, 'Fuck off'. They offered me a lift again, I tell them to, 'Fuck off'. And went on my merry little way drunk as a skunk. Soon the police arrive, I am breathalysed, and it went red before I blew into it. The policeman suggests I sit in the car and drink his coffee hoping that no one can relieve him as all the house alarms are going off. Unfortunately, it's not long before another police car arrives and we're off to the station. I am breathalysed again – feeling more sober now, as I begin to understand what is happening. This time you can see how much over the limit I am, approaching six times over. I was asked to stop blowing. They didn't want to know how it was going to go. I was charged and eventually able to leave around 6:00am. The original police officer offered me a lift home as he was finishing. We chatted about the consequences of what I'd done, and agreed it could have ended up much worse. Once we got to my house the same officer asked me if I would like to go for a drink with him, lol, I declined.

I did a deal with a solicitor. I would recommend a client to his conveyancing team and he would represent me for free. Six times over the limit would not be looked on favourably. I also wanted to keep the car until Christmas was over. He told me to plead not guilty and the case would be adjourned. I did that and on the 6th January I was banned for eighteen months and received a £500 fine. In work I was allocated a driver as I covered three offices and normally drove a company car.

It's March the following year and I am going to hospital to be sterilised. The girls in my office set me a task. Quiet simply – get a date with a doctor, and we will pay for dinner and drinks next time we all go out.

Not being one to look a gift horse in the mouth I accepted the challenge. Here I am at the hospital checking in, admitted to the day ward and it's my turn, I'm still thinking of how I'm going to make this happen when in walks the anaesthetist, introduces himself to me, seemed like very pleasant middle eastern doctor, we chatted and laughed, operation done, I'm woken up by him, I've had a bad reaction to the anaesthetic. I am strapped to the bed he said I kept trying to get off and the straps were there for my safety. He then sang a funny song and we chatted a little more. I knew then this was my victim, I am taken back to the ward, but this time I get a side room, he comes to see me before leaving the hospital, tells me he is going back to his home country for three weeks, makes sure I know his name and off he trots.

The next day my friend Melanie picked me up, I told her about my challenge, and it was decided that I should send him a thank you note with my contact details on. Three weeks later and the phone rings. My daughter calls me, 'Mummy there's a foreign gentleman on the phone I don't understand his name.' I'm smiling now and yes sure enough it was him. 'Hello, how are you?' Thanking me for the card. We chat for a while and arrange to go for a drink. On the day of the meeting I called my drinking buddy Melanie and we drank vodka in the garden. It was a beautiful sunny day and the girls were with their dad. I choose a simple, smart casual outfit to wear. When he arrived, I found myself having to hold on to the door frame – oh one too many drinks. He drove a black Capri – his pride and joy he informed me, a classic car – personally I hated it. We drove past his friend's restaurant so he could see me, and we went to a nice spa hotel with a restaurant and bar for a couple of drinks. I was a bit smashed, so I thought an early night was in order. Task complete, dinner and drinks in hand with the girls, who would have thought we would stay together for six years.

When we met, he used to have a whisky and a small cigar, after his private practice on Wednesday evenings. I would consume copious amounts of alcohol. He would have a couple of small beers at the weekend. He was a Muslim when it suited him. By the time we finished he was drinking two bottles of whisky a week, smoking five small cigars a day, and belly dancing on the coffee table until he fell through it one night. Oh, what a laugh! We learnt so much from each other. But were not good for one another. He finally went home and got an arranged marriage, which has since ended.

As a group of financial consultants we went out for the annual Christmas soiree, we managed to get ourselves barred from the Warrington Gentlemen's Club and McDonald's on the same morning. With a complete free bar, all the staff gone home, we ran amock, likes kids in a candy shop. There were men and women getting it on under the snooker table, in the broom cupboard, ladies and gents loos, everyone was out of control. When the cleaners arrived at 7:00am the next morning, they were banging on the door. We locked them out shouting from the windows, 'Go away!' And them shouting, 'We are calling the police!' Who promptly arrived and evicted us from the building. We are dazed by the morning winter sun – all in black tie dress – we decide to make our way to McDonald's where we were refused service and told to leave. So here we were responsible IFAs drunk on the streets of Warrington behaving badly.

I finally decided to leave as it became too much with a driver. I could not always get to my appointments because I covered three offices.

I rang DHSS to find out what I would get if I did not have a job. Once I knew they would pay my mortgage I left, lived on benefits, went to university, and started cleaning, not just any old house though, one was a merchant banker's, and the other owned a huge golf club, and was a landowner in Cheshire.

Certificates

Carmen

Certificates. I've got quite a few. Let me tell you about my first ever one I got when I was in the convent. I WAS 15 YEARS OLD. It was for ballroom dancing. The Quick Step, Waltz, Foxtrot and Cha Cha dances. Months and months of training with Mother Consolata and the other girls that were in the competition. Traveling to London on the train from Staplehurst, then on the tube.

We arrive at the venue, a big ballroom, where we changed into our costumes and dance shoes. Had our makeup done. Got our numbers pinned to our costumes ready to be called. We danced with each other as we didn't have boy partners. I can't remember what our outfits and shoes were like, I remember it was a day full of dancing, it went in a blur.

I got a first in the Cha Cha which was a gold medal and certificate, 3rd in the Waltz, Quick Step and Foxtrot. We received our medals on the day and our certificates by post. Funny I can't remember how I felt? But my love of music and dance are still with me today. What I do remember is when I danced it took me somewhere beautiful the way we flowed and glided across the floor.

Me aged forty-seven off to City College Northenden. Nail course. Enrolled. I'm the oldest pupil on the course, it's a year course, one night a week. It was hard but I really enjoyed it, Assignments, course work, practical. The first six months were manicure and pedicure, practical and theory, getting our uniform and kit, and a sense of importance. I started sitting at the back of the class and worked my way to the front. The next part of the course was nail extensions more assignments homework and practical on clients. At the end of the course was graduation at the Manchester Town Hall, nervous, happy, excited, proud. Name called: Carmen Jones Level 3 NAIL TECHNICIAN, walk up on to the podium shake hands with the dean, handed a pretend certificate, disappointed no cap and gown. The tutor who took our course was new and learning. I got asked if I would like to enrol for the next term – a beauty course, said yes, enrolled, did a test, passed. For the coming September, again oldest on the course, this was on a different level, there were three levels 1,2,3 enrolled for all of them. It was in 2002.

Completed level 2 in June 2004. National Vocational QUALIFICATION Beauty Therapy. Completed level 3 in July 2005. I got Student of the Year. Got awarded a Certificate of Achievement. Cap and gown. I'm so proud, my family cheering and clapping. I did it. I was 50 years old. I was then asked to teach at one of the City Colleges where I had studied. At the Forum Wythenshawe. The course was N.C.F.E. Certificate of Attendance April 2007 NORTHERN COUNCIL FOR FURTHER EDUCATION.

January 2008 Level 3 Award Pettals [preparing to teach in the lifelong learning sector.] This is where self-confidence takes over or lack of, and I don't follow on to complete my full teaching certificate, THE FEAR OF FAILING. So I take the role of manageress at Sundays Beauty LTD, until March 2019

Several months later I OPEN MY OWN BUSINESS 'BEAUTY by KALMS'. Lots more CERTIFICATES for so many more different courses, always keep your skills updated, still studying for two more courses at present, closed due to COVID-19. LET'S SEE WHERE THESE take me??? Also did an interview for the College Magazine when I was a student – with photograph. I will show you girls when we can meet up again.

WOW I've achieved a lot. SMILING and PROUD XXXXX

Who In Their Right Mind Sets Out To Be A Single Mum

Tia

I know I didn't set out to do it alone. And although you see yourself as a strong woman who couldn't give a flying fuck about being a single mum that society looks down on, it's a lie. You do on a level give a fuck, because you have to find the energy of proving yourself to others. As well as doing well for your race and always having to present yourself in the best light, you have to prove to the world that you're a good mum as well. I suppose the Gruffalo also feels the need to do his race well and break the stereotype of black men as absent or useless fathers. There I go again. Tormenting myself and over analyzing his actions and trying to understand him but I don't think he ever afforded me the same courtesy.

I'm just calling the year 2020, COVID. But instead of 'co' for corona, it's 'co' for courage. Instead of 'vi' for virus, it's 'vi' for victory and instead of 'd' for disease, it's 'd' for dare to be.

It was November 2011. Gruffalo occasionally came in the house after dropping the boys back. I'd done the Christmas shop for toys and presents and I was adamant in my mind that this year he wasn't going to throw me a few quid and say, 'Can you say they are from me too?' I'm not normally that arsey. Some would say, at least he gave you something for them. I get that. But I'd had three years of him passing negative comments of what I had bought my first son, who isn't his, and so now I thought I would just go it alone.

I asked Gruffalo to come upstairs to see the presents I had bought. He smiled and before he got to say his usual line, I quickly got it in, 'So, this is what I bought and I'm just showing you so you don't buy the same but give you an idea of what else to get.' His face dropped. Indirectly I had told him you're not just bunging me some money. This year you're going it alone too on the shopping front.

The uncomfortable silence was interrupted by my youngest kicking off downstairs with his big brother. He wanted a packet of fruit pastilles my friend had left. Gruffalo wanted his kids healthy. I get that. He wants the best for them because he loves them. I appreciate, welcome and respect that. What I didn't appreciate was that we were all on eggshells when he was around trying to do that. We even pretended like we didn't know what sweets and chocolate were when he was around. But a three-year-old will always be in their authentic state of being. No pretending. Just plain old kicking off until they get what they want.

My eldest shouts up the stairs, 'Mum, he's still kicking off.'

Gruffalo snaps straight away, 'Don't give him any sweets.'

I'm feeling tense as my own chest inflates and I watch the Gruffalo's do the same. We lock eyes. He is already well and truly pissed off that I've shown him the presents and good God, now he knows there are sweets in the house, you know, the house where the kids actually live, who knows what's coming next. He growls that he's, 'Getting off.' My son asks me what should he do. I follow Gruffalo who is stampeding down the stairs. My son looks scared.

I shout to Gruffalo, 'Don't snap at him like that and I tell you what go and tell your own son he is not having sweets and then stick around and listen to him bawling.'

Gruffalo ignores the instruction and snaps, 'Oh, do what you want, Dante. You lot always do!'

I see the stress in my son's eyes, and it cuts me. I jump to my weapon of defence that always hurts Gruffalo – swearing. 'Don't fucking talk to my son like that!' My protest to the Gruffalo is borne out of the fact that he never has a nice, calm exchange of words with him and this hurts, because my lad is the sweetest, calmest kid in this world, and I brought a Gruffalo into it.

I predict what's coming next. Gruffalo is going to slam my door as it's not the first time he's charged off like a rhino. I know it's only a matter of time before one day he breaks the glass panel in it. So, I reach over his shoulder to grab the door and I finish my swearing campaign by saying, 'And don't slam my fucking door!'

All the kids are in the hallway. The next thing I know I'm shoved against the wall by a grab of a hand turned fist shoved into my throat. 'I'm sick of you swearing at me in front of my kids!' he hissed.

I instantly start fighting with him. The kids are probably screaming but I am concentrating on hurting him physically, as he has me. I was sick too. Sick of him, who doesn't live with us, scaring us in our own home. My son who was aged thirteen at the time who had not had a fight in his life begins punching the Gruffalo and tells him to get off his mum. This is the sweet boy who shopkeepers would give free stuff to because he was one the most polite kids in the area. No one in his world was ever mean until Gruffalo came into his life.

I continue exchanging blows with Gruffalo and then I notice the Gruffalo is growling my son's name. For a second after that I'm successfully beating the crap out of him but it's because Gruffalo has stopped fighting and demanding I look at my son. My faithful old dog, Lola, has joined in the battle. When I heard the words, 'Look at your son.' I thought he was having a moment of clarity and was suggesting we don't fight in front of his kids. No, he doesn't mean that. He says, 'Look at your son. I've punched him!' The fucker had punched my boy, my sweet boy square in the face. Dazed him and then nearly knocked him out. The dog knew instinctively that we were in danger and began tearing into Gruffalo's shins. He yelled at me to call the dog off. I had no regard. I wasn't going to do that. I was in full on vengeance mode. Between myself and our Lola we have managed to do a good number on him. I've torn down his face but paid the price from a before and after blow to the ribs. Another lashing out by me results in receiving punches to parts of my body he has already struck. Another to the side of the head and I feel dizzy and then he kicks my dog so hard that she yelps and stays down. I drive with all my might and manage to shove the Gruffalo out of the door, screaming, 'You've punched my son and you're going to fucking die!'

The door shuts. He doesn't bang to be let back in. There are cries that echo all around me. I don't know who to comfort first. 'It's OK. It's Ok,' I say as I try to scoop them all up in a hug. But it's not OK. It's so not OK. 'Where's the phone?' I ask. 'Where's the phone? He's going to pay for this!'

I pick up the house phone and I dial my eldest son's dad's number. The only number I know off by heart because he's had it for over twenty years. I'd have struggled to remember anyone's number in what feels like an earth-shattering moment. There's no answer. I go to ring again. Dante's dad would know it was urgent, but before I let it ring long enough for him to answer, I put the receiver down. I'm thinking what would be the outcome if I get Dante's dad involved? He'd probably kill the Gruffalo having hurt his child. Dante will have no dad. My two youngest will have no dad. No winners in that scenario. I pick the phone back up and dial 999.

At this moment in time, I am resentful that I have older brothers on my dad's side but at this time in my life they're not really around in my world. I'm thinking Gruffalo wouldn't be throwing his weight around if I had male relatives keeping an eye. I have no one. Just the police and I wrestle in my mind with the idea of calling the police on a black man. But I need help and enough is enough.

The police come......actually, trained pretty well, in domestic violence. They take photos of my injuries. They take photos of my son's. This is so difficult to watch. This shouldn't have happened to him. I'd somehow managed to get the three and four-year-old to bed. The dog won't leave mine and Dante's side. She became true family that day.

The police tell me that even if I change my mind about prosecuting, it will still go ahead because Gruffalo has assaulted a child. I won't change my mind. But the police have probably seen these things collapse time and time again. I'm good with them taking it in hand. The police also tell me they can arrest him now or do it while he's at work. I have to walk around with a black eye and cauliflower ear and my son has to go to school with physical and emotional bruising, so I figure the Gruffalo being humiliated in public is the least he deserves.

An injunction is granted and with it I immediately feel a little safer. The court case is to be January 31st, only six weeks later. My sister comes with me; the calm, stable one of the family, but even she is livid with what has happened against her nephew and big sister.

I give my evidence. The Gruffalo's brief is a complete arsehole. I'm stood like a witch in the stocks or on a platform with a noose. He makes me repeat the words I said before the physical altercation. 'Don't' talk to my son like that.' He reminds me I'm under oath and that I swore. He makes me repeat the whole sentence and address it to the magistrates directly. I know exactly what he's trying to do. He thinks my embarrassment of having to swear at the magistrates will cause me to be defensive. Somehow, I'm less of a victim if I have a great big unfeminine sweary mouth. I speak. 'I feel a fraud stood here because I have a criminology degree. I know how women are judged on their femininity and that a woman stood here crying can win over the courts. I can't cry today. I've cried enough. I did swear and I do swear, and I did cry and what I said was, 'Don't fucking talk to my son like that!' I'm tired of not running my household comfortably, the way I want to. It's why I left him.'

The magistrates said, 'That will be all.' My brief was up next. She said I could stay but I didn't want to be in there a moment longer. I told my sister to stay to hear what Gruffalo had to say.

It felt like forever, but it wasn't that long. My sister returned and gave me a big hug. She said my brief was amazing. I'd only met her that morning whereas Gruffalo had had his for a few weeks covering every little detail. The injuries or lack of them that Gruffalo had received was how my brief got to put the noose on his neck. He had only one picture of where I had clawed his face, which had come after him hitting my son. She asked how he had defended himself from me. He put his hands up. She remarked on his unclenched fist and limp hands. She asked him again. Then she mimicked his actions and said, 'So, you were more like a cat pawing at a ball of string?' That was the line that won. There was no way his limp hands could have caused the injuries he had to my son, so Gruffalo had hung himself in his lies.

Two weeks later I receive a call from the police to inform me of the full outcome of the court's decision and sentence. Gruffalo is given a £500 fine, a nine-month compulsory attendance at a domestic violence awareness course, a three-year injunction, and two years suspended sentence. This was all to take place from February the 14th. The best Valentine's present I've ever had and one he probably won't forget either.

So, during all the shit, which is what Mancunians are calling the pandemic of COVID-19, I like many of us have been tested. It's also been a test of who we give a shit about and also who gives a shit about us. So, this week I've been visited by the ghosts of lovers past. Danny dropped off and ran after bringing me a box of surgical gloves, three bottles of sanitizer and a ten pack of gardening gloves. The last item shows he knows me well. Dante's dad came and dropped me money for food shopping. Not just for his son [who is now a man] but also for the two kids that are not his, because he knows I'm out of work after being made redundant at the start of lockdown. He probably also knows kids do not have school bellies when they are at home. They eat on average every ninety minutes.

I bigged Dante's dad up on Facebook. He himself is not on Facebook and neither is the Gruffalo, but I knew someone would see the post. Plus, it's good I think to show people that exes can be decent and do the right thing. One of Gruffalo's friends inferred that Gruffalo hadn't been helping financially. I did the decent thing and pointed out that he does contribute financially; it's just that he wouldn't dream of giving me something extra like a bag of shopping or ask did we need anything, especially in a time like this. You know how it goes, Facebook AKA farcebook, someone let Gruffalo know what I had said. He called me. He said why couldn't we have a relationship where he could be more involved in a positive way. He did his usual twisting around and justifying his own negative reactions. I could tell he was dying to bring up what I'd written on Facebook and the fact that I had always respected Dante's dad. But he didn't go there as he would then have to reveal who the snoop source was on Facebook. I must have been assertive for once because I confidently batted everything he said, back to him. He had the cheek to ask who I was showing off in front of. I told him to FaceTime me to show him I was alone. He didn't. I took from that suggestion of me 'showing off' that I had finally thrown off the shackles of being his inferior, his victim, his oppressed prey.

This week I have found my courage, my victory and finally I dare to be me.

The Predator

Catherine

It's the evening after the night before, still hung over from the Reno, music and one too many drinks. Ah! Here comes our next victim, or was he? I'm walking with Margaret in Withington, we both want to go for a drink but cash is low, we could go to the pub as we have done many times and find someone to buy us a drink or two, at seventeen you don't give a shit and you are almost fearless. However, before our eyes came the Predator, driving a clapped out Ford Zephyr with reggae music blasting out the window even though it was late and cold. Two black men pull alongside us. We were almost juveniles they were old men. They asked us what we were doing. We all chat a while, they invite us in the car and we all went for a drive, and free drinks all night. If I knew then what now I know the following sequence of events would not have happened.

We are in the car. The guys are not easy on the eye although they were pleasant enough. We go for a drink; I cannot remember where. We did not stay in the pub for long as we were tired and had work the next day. Predator took his friend home, then my friend, he was charming and well spoken and old. Let us get this into perspective. He was probably fifty we were barely seventeen. He told us he was thirty-seven. He took my number and called me a few days later. We went out for dinner to a steak house in town. I told him I wanted to go to Rafters afterward (Mike Shaft is the DJ). He took me although he hated it, and I didn't really care, time goes by and this guy is working on me although I still thought I was playing him. I'm seeing him on a regular basis now, my friend Margaret doesn't understand, she has moved in with a guy who lived in Hulme who I introduced her to. He is a Jamaican guy who beats women just because he can. I am dipping in and out with the Predator and seeing another guy as well. Margaret's fella and the Predator did not like the Reno, they never went there, they did not like Margaret and myself going, they were insecure, and too old. Predator often took me to the Russell Club; he was still paying for everything. I was wild and a free spirit.

Mum and I have fallen out again and I had nowhere to live I end up staying at his love nest, in Longsight. It's a bedsit with everything you would need for a one-night stand.

I decided to move in as it seems to offer me more freedom than mum's. It was around this time we started sleeping together. That was hot, better than I had ever known or thought possible. Still giving me my freedom, little did I know he was a pimp and had several other girls on the go giving him money, which he then spent on me. Ok so now I am in the flat happy I think I can come and go as I please.

The Stylistics are coming to Manchester and I get a ticket for my friend Christine and myself. We arrive at the Free Trade Hall long before the show starts, sitting waiting patiently, a guy came over introduces himself as Jack, chats a while, asks if we would like to meet the group after the show? Hell Yes!!! He tells us to wait in our seats until everyone has gone, he will send someone over for us, I know I am not going to miss the chance to meet Herb Morel and Russell Thompkins Jnr. I'll sit there all day. The show finishes and here we go, we are introduced to the group, their band, and Kool and the Gang, who were on tour with them, I am in seventh heaven cannot believe this. There is a bit of a party going on at the Midland Hotel which we are invited to.

The next day we are off to Dunstable, touring like groupies with the Stylistics and crew, I went back to the bedsit to get some stuff told Predator where I was going he was very angry however

I didn't give a shit, I am off to Dunstable I told him, with that got in a cab, waved, passed by mum's to pick a few bits up. She too was not happy but I was off. What a trip – Dunstable, London, Glasgow, Edinburgh, back to Manchester we were away for one week, such fun, turns out Jack owns Kennedy Street Enterprise, which was the company that arranged for black music artists to tour the UK from the States. He never did anything untoward and let me run free just checked in with me to make sure I was ok like a father figure. We stayed in touch for a couple of years.

Back in Manchester, can't go home, so the bedsit it is. Predator is there really mad, I think this was the first time I saw his angry jealous aggressive streak, however he has a bigger agenda so moves on quickly. I tow the line but decide to move out of the bedsit. I find a room in a shared house in Stretford full of middle-class young ladies, and then me ha ha. I love it here and get a job in the offices of Goblin Food, from where I brought freebies home for dinner most nights. Before I know it, Predator has convinced me we should have a baby and I finally become pregnant, I was weak, and him deep rooted in my psyche now I just do as I am told. It's difficult to explain when someone takes over your mind, body and soul; this is done slowly so you are not even aware of it until it is too late and you are trapped.

In August 1976 we have a son together one of three born to him that year, one to his wife I had no idea they were still together, I found out he still claims benefits for all her fourteen children from her house. The other was a girl who I knew nothing about, I think it was her first to him, but she had other children.

Whilst I was in hospital, our son was born jaundiced and small, so I was there for ten days. Both my mum and I notice when he visited me with my friend Christine, they seem overly comfortable together. Predator was always prowling looking for his next conquest, and here she was. She had been in care all her life. Both Christine and her two sisters were abandoned by their mother, and found naked, in a white pram on a piece of wasteland in Longsight seventeen years earlier. A tragic story which her foster mother told her. She showed her the newspaper clippings, of how she was abandoned. Christine was clearly vulnerable and an easy target for the Predator. We met in a care home on Darley Avenue in Didsbury, this was a beautiful place run by nuns, we all had our own room it was clean, warm and caring. We earned pocket money, and I went to college. Everyone came from dysfunctional homes, but we all got on. There was seven of us in the house. When Christine was old enough, she came to live in my shared house. Once I got home I found the Predator passing my room to get to hers, then back to mine WTF he had no shame, he also started telling me about women who gave him money and how much they loved him, they bought him cars, jewellery and gave him cash, in turn he slept with them and ruled their lives. He suggested I do the same and wanted to send mine and Christine's pics to an agency. I didn't do it and he would get angry and often just slapped me. He would come to mine being depressed as he had no money and suggested I didn't love him because a true love would go out and work for him.

A lady came to live in the house, her name was Margot, she was much older than us worked in the kitchen at Kellogg's, she had been around the block and told me stories of the Nile Club she went to and the strokes she picked up, one day she met the Predator she could not hide the fact that he was one of her strokes, she also told me he had gone to prison in the 60s for living off immoral earnings, apparently it was a really big case in Manchester and some of the girls went to court supporting him.

I was bringing my son up on my own he was cheating in the very same house as me with my no longer friend, as I had confronted her and caught them together on more than one occasion, he beat me badly that night and told her she was not allowed out of her room, only to cook and use the bathroom. She eventually moved out. Six months later I get a council flat in Sale Moor, my son is in full time nursery and I have a part time job in a bar he was still coming around. We occasionally slept together and he did odd jobs for me. He still got angry and aggressive if I went out or worked nights. He would often be waiting for me hiding in the gutter like a slug where he would attack me for no reason. I managed to get my life on track – could buy some bits for my flat, made new friends and had an affair with the singer in the bar. Lol that was funny.

My life was getting a bit easier, Predator was not hitting me as often. He doesn't come around that much. He begins to understand I cannot stand him. I've changed my place of work now and have a bar job in Salford I know the person who owns the bar which is why I moved.

Here comes Mr Proctor he walks into the bar one afternoon, all tanned, tall, handsome extremely funny, casual but well dressed, we start chatting, he comes in every afternoon as he is back from a trip at sea being an engineer in the Merchant Navy. He always tips me talks shit but is funny. The Predator and I were no longer seeing each other, one afternoon Mr Proctor offers me a lift home I let him drop me off at the nursery, my son was a handful and I didn't want to upset his routine. Mr Proctor gives me a lift home one evening. My sister was babysitting and as we get to the gate out jumps Predator hitting Mr Proctor across the back with a piece of wood then attacking me, telling me he will kill me. My sister calls the police. He and Proctor are fighting in the garden, when the police arrive. They want to charge Predator, but I'm too scared and Mr Proctor found him amusing. And now I have to deal with the aftermath where I am told by Predator I have to give up my job, but I've grown strong now and didn't listen to his shit.

A few days later I am on the bus taking my son to nursery there is a baby crying, mum was clearly distressed. I turned to see if I could help, there before my eyes was Christine. We just stared at each other. My heart broke for her – she is now a victim but not a strong one. I help her with the baby and cried inside for her. She had just come out of the hospital after taking an overdose. She cried, told me she was sorry, I said it did not matter. He was treating her badly, she lost weight, her beauty was gone, she was broken. We swapped numbers. I had to get off the bus. Feeling sad all day I was scared to call her in case he was at the house. I knew what he would do to her if he found out we were in touch with each other.

A week or so later she called me from the hospital. She had tried again to take her life, she was desperate and asked if I would come and see her. I agreed and bought her a bottle of Ribena. The evening I was supposed to go she called me, said they had let her go home and she would be in touch. I felt something was wrong but had no way of finding out. Now what happened has stayed with me for the whole of my life. Predator called me. He said Christine had taken her life. She had fed the baby, wrapped him up then gone into the bathroom and hung herself. Just writing this makes me cry. She, a beautiful young vulnerable woman with a tiny baby was pushed to her limit by that pig. She was nineteen years old,, he was in his fifties for fuck sake, how could this happen, I can't believe it. I feel faint, angry, sad, that fucking lowlife has done this to her. I told him to fuck off don't call me again. He had also found out we had been talking to each other. After this he is back on my case, hiding in bushes, jumping on me, attacking me, beating me, threatening to kill me, and Mr Proctor. He is demanding to see my son, who was difficult and did not need any more disruption. He came to my house one night after work, with a hammer smashing everything in sight, threatening to kill me, my sister. Somehow I managed to grab my son, we run out on the street, a black cab passes, we flag it down. By now he has caught up with us. He is holding onto the door swinging from side to side like a deranged mad man, trying to pull my son out of the cab. The taxi driver kept going, he's shouting at him telling him to get off the cab and he calls the police, but finally he falls off.

We go to mum's. I cannot go back to that flat. Proctor has gone back to sea. I am alone now. We are at mum's who is tolerating us, my son is becoming more and more difficult, breaking everything he could and why wouldn't he? I was a bad mum with no parenting skills or role models to help me, and I am dealing with this shit. Predator is still jumping out of bushes telling me he won't stop until he gets his son. Mum and I are walking home one evening when I am hit over the head then dragged along the road. My mum screams at him, 'Fecking bastard I'll kill you!' She attacks him with her umbrella and manages to knock him to the ground. He lets me go, then mums starts to kick the shit out of him. I'm not sure how we got home that evening or what happened after that. We were both clearly shaken by the level of violence Predator had shown us.

Now Mr Proctor's ex-wife has found out where I live. She would sit outside mum's house waiting for me, following in her mini shouting out the window, 'Nigger lover! Get back to the ghetto!' Often with her eight-year-old son in the car. This all became too much for mum, and quiet rightly – she had her own shit to deal with. My eldest sister was going on holiday and said we could stay at her house for a couple of weeks, so I packed my bags took my son and moved. My younger sister was also living there at the time. One night Predator came with an axe threatening to smash the house up. We called the police, but he got away. The police were kind and funny but there was nothing they could do unless I pressed charges. I was too scared.

Life was horrendous. I wasn't working, Predator kept turning up, son had wrecked my sister's house – my fault for being a bad mum, and unable to take control of this situation. I was not coping at all. My sister comes back, she cannot believe her house, it was awful. We go back to my mum's, she cannot cope. He's on the prowl all the time, she's following us in the car, son is running amok. I'm on the verge of a breakdown, mum doesn't want my son there, Proctor is back, he and mum are telling me to give my son up, give him to his dad he needs to be with his own – by this they meant colour. My head is spinning, I'm full of rash, I don't know where to turn. My mum says my son can no longer stay there, with Proctor backing her. They are in my head, 'He needs to be with his own,' I hear it all the time, 'Give him to his dad. If you don't your life will be full of misery.'

I contact the social services tell them my story, they advise temporary foster parents, just around the corner from where we live. He is not a bad child; no child is bad it's just bad parenting. I learnt this years later. I am trapped don't know what to do. Predator has stolen everything I own in the flat and taken it to his wife's house. Proctor helps me financially but has gone back to sea. After another beating from Predator, my mum telling me to give my son to his dad, Proctor still agreeing with her, I have no help no support, I finally hand him over. I did not look at either of them. Now my heart is broken. Mum seems to think this is ok, and Proctor agrees. Neither of them considered the impact this would have on me, or my son. Predator has now got two new children to take care of – my son and Christine's son. He takes them both to another lady, who also had a son to him and a daughter to his friend – which happened when he was in prison. Predator has around thirty children dotted around Manchester.

When he died. I found out his age. He was older than my mum. Even after this incident he continues his pursuit of young victims without shame or remorse.

Boy's Not Mine

Carmen

The year is 1987. LB and I going through one of the worst times of our married life. We weren't really living together. He's over in Stockport with some tart. I can't remember her name. He comes here to drop off money for the kids and to see what I'm doing. I'm out a lot, drinking a lot. I know he was seeing someone, someone else, also Joan over in Moston. Fast forward to New Year's Eve 1987. New Year's Eve party. I know LB will be there at some time. I'm going with our P. The kids are taken care of. I'm getting ready, new outfit, vodka while I'm getting ready, meet our P.

Go over to Whalley Range. The party is in full swing, I'm waiting to see if he will turn up. He does, we are very aware of each other. My heart beats faster still after all these years I can remember. I'm drunk but sober, he's going he says, 'Goodbye'. I can't leave it so I follow him outside. I remember we embrace and I'm sure we say we love each other. He says, 'See ya bye.'

And I say, 'Congratulations on the birth of your son on Christmas Eve.'

He turns and says, 'Thanks, there was another son born six weeks ago.'

Screams. It's me. I throw a punch, follow him to his car and kick it. Anger, hurt, sick; these are all the feelings I'm feeling. He drives off, I go back to the party. Raging I'm asking who knew about these babies. Family knew. Baby number one is to a woman called J. You know I know her; she is a cousin to a really good friend of mine. She wasn't someone I socialised with. He and her met through friends. Baby number two, mother from Moston, had a daughter who I later found out calls LB dad. K was born on Christmas Eve. Let's get back to NYE 87 into 1988. I get absolutely smashed. New Year's Day I'm going to P's dad's with the kids for dinner and having a family day there. I'm so hungover and upset. Angry. I'm in a terrible state. I'm that bad they put me in a bath, I can't swallow I'm panicking. I go home with the kids. I end up in the MRI hospital, I think I'm dying, it turns out I've got alcohol poisoning. I go home and take to my bed for days (about two), I hate him, I hate them. Truthfully, I still love him with all my heart. I'm hurting I'm angry. February, a knock on the door, police, a warrant to search the house. He has been arrested for drugs. At the time he is living with one from Stockport after a fashion, because he was seeing someone from Chorlton. She was the other woman. He gets bail, gets picked back up again, they raid the house in Stockport. Bang to rights. She says it's his. In court he gets remanded. No bail. Court date. She tries to wind me up. I warn her don't mess with me. In court address read out, she is down as his common-law-wife, I'm raging.

Sentencing. She gets three months. He gets three years. As he is going down, he turns, looks at me and says, 'I love you.' I have to go home and tell the kids that dad got three years in jail. The best friends that he walked with at the time, were to look after the kids and me. A little allowance each week, spends for the kids. The VO started coming. I hadn't forgotten baby mothers. JH didn't really exist for me as I didn't know where she lived, she stayed under the radar. Joan was something else. She was in touch with LB and some of the family. One day I was at a family home with the kids, and I noticed a photo and I knew it was one of the boys, turns out it was baby No.2. I'm not sure who brought the photo to the house. Well, me being me decided I was going to find out where she lived, and go there to see her face to face. Which I did. At first, she wouldn't let me in, eventually she did. Wow was I surprised. I asked her how long had she and LB been seeing each other. On the next visit to see him we had a massive row about me going to her house and what I'd said to her and done. He banned me from the prison and visits. Told me to leave her alone, that she was a nice girl and didn't deserve it. Yeah right that's why she had an affair with a married man. And I wonder what tale he spun her? One thing I did think about was that he was a habitual womaniser. How in the end I told him to go, it hurt so much. How we are together is sometimes a mystery. When he got sentenced, I went wild for a short time but I survived. I never sit in judgment of anyone. There is more: the visits, the home leave, the getting out for good, the doubts. The daughter who has the same birthday as one of the boys, who turned detective to find him. The visits from K and his sister. Our kid's reactions. How life works out. Life on the outside. Habits and drink. Saying enough is enough.

Madness, Magnets and Mamma

Tia

Answering the question, or maybe just exploring it, as I'm going into this with a free hand and mind, but does having a mentally ill mother build character? I've thought a lot about my mum lately. I probably think about her at least a moment every day since she's been gone. Sometimes it's just a fleeting thought, sometimes it's a long daydream or the best ones are when she comes to me in a dream. Consciously, I have my thoughts about my mum, that are like the ends of a magnet, they are charged positively and sometimes negatively depending on how I'm feeling. But when I dream about her it's actually never negative. It's like a comfort.

I've just had an hour's catnap. I've been good – getting up at daft o'clock and going for a run at 6:00am most mornings. I was cold when I got back in and tired and I decided I was going to have another hour in bed. I stuck my dressing gown on, tied my belt and put my hood up looking a bit like little Red Riding Hood when I catch myself in the mirror. I'm asleep but it's like I'm wide-awake because I'm dreaming but it feels so real.

'Feel that; feel how hard my leg muscles are,' I say. I look at the person I'm asking and it's my mum. But she looks about ten years younger, about the age I am now. She's in a pair of Adidas tracksuit bottoms. This is a real memory stored in my mind because when my mum was alive, she was always a big girl who tried to hide her size under tent like skirts and nighties: she had once taken my stepdad's jog pants and put them on and came into my room to ask my opinion. She never ever asked my opinion. She was the one who stated instructions and barked commands. But she's come in my room being nice. This usually signals alarm bells because I'm not used to her being nice but this day I'm enjoying the fact that she's doing something out of her comfort zone and wants me as her safe zone.

'Your legs look thin in trousers mum. You should wear them more often.'

'Do you think so?' She says.

'Yeah. I don't know why you only wear skirts.'

She quips back, 'Same as I don't know why you don't.' And she has a point as I'm rarely in a skirt. In my dream she's in the jog pants, larger than life and this time she looks comfortable in them, almost as if she's been working out, exercising in them. I feel her squeeze my thigh muscle.

'Oh yeah,' she says, 'Feel mine!'

I feel hers and I think where has all the fat gone and who would've thought we'd be working out comparing muscles. I wake up and like a mad cow I reach for my thighs to see if they are as muscular as they were in my dream. Ha ha they're not. But I give them a gentle pat, to tell them, 'Soon though, they're coming soon.' Then I remember, I've dreamt of my mum. It makes me smile for a second and then I hear a notification beep on my phone and when I look on WhatsApp, someone has sent me a meme which says, 'Weird moms build character.' Like my dream, it feels like a message, a message from my mum. I'd had a friend on the allotment tell me the day before that she was attracted to madness, and chaos, 'mess' was the word she used. It immediately made me think of my mum. She always had crazy, unstable friends and came from a crazy, unstable family so her chances of also being a little crazy were high.

Whilst working with school kids I used to have a saying, 'You have to be a little bit crazy to survive in this world!' And I would say it in my best Russian accent, and they would all laugh. Looking back, I said it because I knew some of these kids had bonkers parents too and like a magnet, I was drawn to them as much as they were to me. So, in all honesty I think I was prepping them all for the future. Throwing in a warning but glazing it over with a bit of humour because God knows they're going to need that too.

Intuition used to be my trick of my toolbox of survival, until I read a book, *The Daughters of Narcissistic Mothers*, and I found that it wasn't some magic intuition that I had, but the ability to pick up on peoples' vibrations from very young; what people said but more in tune with how they said it. What they didn't say, as much as what they did. The pauses, the twitches, the restless legs. The long sighs, the stomping, the placing or slamming of things, the silence, and I had been learning it all. I said from as early as I can remember in my own head, there's something not right here; an uneasiness planted in my childhood which crept into adulthood. So, my brain is doing a good job at only allowing me to dream about my mum in a positive light.

During my degree, a social psychology lecturer taught us that we are all cognitive misers. Cognitive equalling thinking and misers, well, equalling a stingy cunt. If I were to show you a marble from a bag and it was white, and another and another, all white marbles one after the other, eventually your mind would stop counting them. But during drawing out the marbles I pulled out a single black one, followed by lots of white marbles again, if I were to ask you how many white marbles were there? You would probably say, there were a lot of white marbles and one black. The same would be said if we switched the colour of the marbles. We can't help but consolidate the info in front of us. And it's a bit like this time with the security guard in Kwik Save, back in the 1980's. He's seeing lots of white marbles and then one black marble. My mum's kids are the black marble. My mum was often miserable with us, but no one could fuck with her kids, because she'd have a go at singlehandedly ripping your head off. She didn't actually do this to the security guard but almost every time we went in with her, she would say to him, 'Come on you daft twat, come and follow me and me 'arfcast kids around like we're thieves while the white heroin addicts are robbing the store blind.' The funny thing was the security guard was black and so there lay some of the confusion for me growing up which definitely came from the environment and not my mixed-race genes. Another memory I have is at my nana's about aged five. I was there most Saturdays if it was a sunny day. Clocking seasonal disorder, that terminology wasn't around then. Another undiagnosed condition to add to my mother's list. At my nana's, my mum is asking my auntie where she'd been going every night. My Auntie Lily lived in the flat below us, a Georgian house with three floors converted into three flats in Whalley Range. Every night I would go down to my auntie's to read to my cousin. There weren't many kids' books but there was this massive textbook filled with words and the odd diagram. I can't read the words but I'm having a good go at it and I'm coming up with words that sound like I'm talking a foreign language. I think I sometimes bored my cousin Donna to death, and I swear she was pretending to go to sleep for me to stop but I can't be sure. My auntie would then give me about 50p in ten pence pieces. I'd be so happy that I had so many coins. Getting a 50p coin just didn't cut it and my auntie was on to that.

After I'd finished reading, I'd go back to my mum's in the flat above but then my mum started to get suspicious of my auntie. Probably because you could hear whenever somebody came in or out of the flats. That Saturday at my nana's I can see my auntie's legs are crossed but her leg is bouncing up and down and causing her foot to kick the air. She takes a big drag of her cigarette and she exhales very long and slow. My mom's chest is heaving up and down. She is holding a cup of tea and tapping it with her finger. They exchange words. I can't remember the words, but I remember seeing the tension on their bodies. My mum accuses her of leaving her kid, 'To go and see ya fucking boyfriend.' My auntie replies with something nasty with the word prostitute. It's after this word my mum's cup of tea takes

on a life of its own and goes west across the living room. The
target is to break the cigarette and I'm hoping not my auntie's
face. The cigarette snaps in half. My auntie is still holding it
but her temper snaps. Nana's nerves have snapped. Nana has
a rug in the middle of the room with all the seating furniture
around the edge. Without even being aware I don't think she has
realized she has set up the perfect wrestling arena. My auntie
is flattened under the weight of my mum. My mum is winning
but I'm not cheering anybody on, but I do feel like nobody is
on her side. My other auntie tries to console me. I'm probably
crying or shouting but I don't remember. My auntie did try but
as she has never hugged me before, not that I remember, it feels
strange, so I push her away and tell her to get off me. That wasn't
the only fight. There was to be another one featuring good old
granddad; the wanderer returns.

Madness is like a magnet. It attracts and it repels.

Home Leave

Carmen

Preparing for his home leave, let's go back just a little, because to get here we have to see how he's coming back home, as when he got locked up, this wasn't his home, well not on paper, according to him it was always home. He told me this when we got back together, in one of our chats. We wrote often to each other, I've still got all the letters, back then you got a visiting order in the post. You would say who wanted to be on the visit and he would request their name to be on the VO order. When he was on remand, he could have a visit every day, once he got sentenced it had to be a VO. From then on it was only me and the kids who requested to visit. We wrote regularly, and we would write about anything, the kids, everyday stuff. He would send birthday cards for the kids and me. I used to send him or I should say get him his newspapers and books, cartoon comics. He would have drawings of me and the kids done from photos I had sent in to him. On birthdays and Christmas, a guy would write verses to put in the cards. He said how he would never get in trouble again, never go back inside. Which he hasn't. As much as I looked forward to his letters he looked forward to mine. The letters are in a cloth holdall that was made in the prison, all the books, letters, photos, cards, letters from whoever wrote to him.

Back to the home leave, it was from the Friday morning until the Sunday teatime. I picked him up in a cab, excited, nervous, laughing, home. It's being cool chilling, a spliff, vodka, champagne. The bedroom, shy, nervous, quick sex.

Bath, bathroom chat, rampant sex. Was it good for you??? Kids home from school and childminder. People passing by. It was a busy boozy weekend. Weird because once he went back to Strangeways, I remember chatting to P and saying I don't know if I wanted us to be together, we had not been together for over two years. I only had to think about my children, not a man, husband, in my everyday life. I went to work a couple of days a week, which I hadn't told him about. I always liked the freedom of not having to think about a man, just the kids. And my way of life. I could please myself what I did. How would the kids react to dad being back home? They were happy, the three older kids knew by now what dad had been up to. The youngest was too young to understand. The next home leave would be for a week. Let's see how that goes? It was a weekend of mixed emotions that didn't come to the surface until he went back inside.

Me And My Mum Are Siamese Twins
Tia

Y ou would read that and think me and my mum were inseparable, solid and full of love for one another. Love is a complex emotion. I don't know if it's like that for everyone; if it's meant to be or if there is an objective, universal definition for it. So, then is love subjective? Do we only ever measure it against our own ideals?

I'll be forty-five this week and I think I'm learning for the first time about self-love. I've been catching myself in the mirror and there she is, my mum, staring back at me, frowning. I fix my face, unfurrow my brow and pout a little like I've actually got a top lip. I wish more of the black side of me had kicked in there. I'll be yelling something to the kids, contradictory, like, 'Stop bloody shouting and come here and speak to me instead of bawling halfway across the house!' And I say this shouting just like she did. My kids laugh at the irony the same way I laughed at my mum. My mum sighing exaggeratingly or occasionally catching some of the contagious laughing and trying to hold down a smile whilst raising an eyebrow as if to say, 'Watch it!' I now do exactly the same.

There's often a strained relationship between mothers and daughters. I wonder if that comes from being so alike and wanting or resenting the choices daughters make before their mothers' eyes?

There are things I have done for my mother that I now regret, and it centers around, identifying, searching, needing and wanting love. I absorbed her pain when she told me traumatic things about her past. It made me angry for her. It made me protect her and even threaten to fight for her. Any time I was in a heated or violent situation with a stranger, the anger always came from a place where I was in my head fighting someone I knew in real life.

It's the late 90s. I'd been in Carrie's Wine Bar on a soul night and I don't know how but I've come to be arguing with an African woman older than me and then I start with her husband who has got involved. I'm threatening to rip his head off and all sorts and shouting all sorts of out of order things like, 'E'ar dickhead, you're in fucking England now, you don't get to boss women around and they just do as their fucking told!' Insult the pair of them at the same time, eh.

Obviously, I've had one too many Bacardis and I think I'm ten-men. Alcohol will do that to ya. That, coupled with underlying unresolved emotional problems. And on the bus home I'm arguing with a white woman, older than me, who is with an African guy around my age, and half her own. My friend is being loud. The guy calls her a slut. I see red and unleash. The mist is down, and my mouth is faster than Road Runner holding a flick knife. My words are cutting, 'Are you fucking stupid? She's the only old fucking slut here!' and I point to the woman twice his age. The guy charges towards me and pushes me. I punch him and he punches me back and there we are swinging left hooks and body blows around the metal bar and getting tangled in the process, grabbing at one another.

The bus driver shouts he has called the police. The woman is screaming, 'You've got fucking issues, you!' The words penetrate me. I knew deep down I did but to hear them out loud does something to you.

It was like an unveiling.

Exposed.

I'm doing what my mum has always done, behaving like a scared dog and becoming vicious in the process. 'You daft old slut. I've got issues? You've got delusional issues. He's only with

105

you for his stay and his fucking green card. Fucking idiot!' There, that's how I dealt with being publicly exposed on my issues. The African guy wants to kill me at this point which is good timing because the police have arrived and no doubt the police will see the angry black man before the mixed-race girl with issues.

I spend an hour or so in the police station giving a statement. And as it's the 90s I don't really think the police can be arsed with a Saturday night drunk and disorderly because I don't remember anything coming of it, but I am left with that woman's words of, 'You've got issues!'

Like Siamese twins, me and my mum for a time are the same person. We want love so much that we request it in the most unloving of ways. Why am I so angry at the two African guys? Well, I was angry that I had a stepdad. Not angry that he was African. I suppose, kind of. I think I've said this before, it was always like he was telling me off all the time. But, in fact it was just his accent. I get it now.

That week, at the age of twenty-one my mum had rung me all upset (she did this often) to tell me that she's had a massive argument with my stepdad. Looking back, I now see how she completely goaded and manipulated me into behaving like a complete psycho. After rambling on about this and that, she finally says, 'And he said when you were fourteen you came in the bedroom and asked him for a tenner and called him daddy.' Now this could sound completely innocent if you were raised right or completely messed up if you weren't. I never, ever called him daddy! I never ever even called my own dad that as a small child. That says a lot too. But I did recall calling my stepdad, 'dad', and not his name, when I wanted something. At the time he didn't have any kids and he's taken my youngest sister on as his own and she called him dad. I knew he loved it. His face would light up when she said it, and she was treated like a little princess for it. So, call it manipulative or genius, I called him dad once to get a tenner out of him.

Seven years later my mum is raging like a banshee telling me some shit down the phone. She said he was still at her house. At the time I'm living on Sedgeborough Road and she's on Greame Street. If I stick my trainers on and give it some legs, I can be at my mum's in about five minutes. I spot a claw hammer in the hallway and I stick it in my jeans.....those jeans with the pockets down the side of the leg like a carpenter so I suppose I don't look too odd carrying a hammer on the street.

My stepdad is outside the shop on Broadfield Road. 'What are you saying? What are you fucking saying to my mum?' Clearly, I'm behaving like I've heard one too many lines from a Gooch or Doddington crew member exchanging words, which was the usual opening line before all hell broke loose. I can't even remember if he replied I just remember me thinking, 'What are you doing? She's manipulated you into doing this.'

I kept having these split-second conscious moments in amongst the red mist episodes that occurred all throughout my twenties. I was following the same path as my mother and getting nowhere fast. I even got into a fight with a guy at uni because he was being sexist and homophobic and my one working class, gay friend looked so hurt and that was it, I was off, wanting to rip the guy's head off.

My mum's proud of me for going to uni and doesn't want me getting into fights because she said, 'One day you'll end up getting arrested!' It's one of the things that she's prided herself on – having all her kids never bring police to the door. She did progress to being proud of us for all going to uni.

It was when I became a mentor that my mum and me began to drift. My studying was now being put to use in an experiential way and I had been sharing some of my case studies with her and you could see I was making sense of my own childhood and it was getting her a little shook.

She began drinking more. She'd always enjoyed a drink but, in the past, it was done when she went out on a weekend. She wasn't going out as much these days, but she was drinking in the house. She told us she had agoraphobia and we knew she'd always suffered with depression. I'd even resigned myself to the idea that the depression thing might have been genetic, rather than situational, as I had struggled with it too. That feeling of wanting to be loved always came in the form of me throwing my mum a couple of hundred quid when I got my student loan. My sister and I had left home, but my mum still had two little ones and was now divorced. I thought I was helping her, but it turns out I was enabling her drinking habit, which was gradually increasing and unbeknown to me, putting my siblings in danger. If I saw my mum in a drunken stupor, it disgusted me. She knew me well and could read my face. It vexed her. This would mean I would face a punishment sometime soon. It usually came in the form of turning up at my door at 3:00am, drunk, crying. I would get dressed, walk her back. She'd then tell me she's not a good mother. I'd have to tell her all the good things she had done for us like: made us go to school, fed us regularly, didn't stick us in care, blah blah blah. She'd tell me she loved me. I'd say it would be nice if you told me that not pissed.

The next day she would say 'I' was a bad mother for leaving my seven-year-old alone while I walked my drunk mother up the road on a two minutes walk! I'd defend myself by saying he was asleep. 'It's five minutes and besides it's better than leaving a ten-year-old with a newborn baby for you to go slagging it down the Nile.' And this continued like this until one day she gave me the final insult through her crazy friend, Mad Pat.

Mad Pat had been prostituting out her mentally ill daughter. I went mad and said some awful things including, 'You've already lost a son to heroin, the least you could do is look after your one daughter.'

Mad Pat replied, 'My son is dead, but I didn't kill mine like you did!' I know exactly what she means, and I knew exactly who had told her.

While at uni, I had started a relationship with a guy. It was good to begin with but then I noticed how jealous he was of my son. I wasn't having it. The final straw was when he punched a wall in frustration and woke my son up. I didn't hang about for a change. Plus, he was an alcoholic, which I only realized when he didn't drink for two days and began to shake with DTs.

My life was hard enough being a single mum, working and studying and I had to weigh up whether I was prepared to be a single mum for a second time and quit uni or stay a single mum to one child and get a degree. I chose the latter and I had a termination. I didn't feel guilty or ashamed until I heard those words from Mad Pat's lips and I didn't feel hurt until my own mother said, 'At least when I meet my maker, I can look him in the eye because I am not a murderer!'

My mum continued with her brutal messages and when I blocked her by phone she moved on to sending me poisoned letters. It went on like this for years. Now and again, I would get a 'Sorry' from her and an invite for dinner, but it would quickly deteriorate again.

I finished uni, met up with Gruffalo and had a couple more kids. My mum didn't really get to know them as well as my eldest. She invited me, my kids, my sister and her kid down to her house in the Easter of 2014. She had moved to a new house again, which told me her mind was still unsettled. I had lost count how many times we had moved to a new house growing up. She promised us she would be sober so my sister and I agreed we would go.

We got to my mum's and no surprise she was drunk. My kids and my sister's kid were only about six and a half, five and four years old. They didn't understand and they didn't know any better, only unquestionable love for their nana, so when she asked them for a hug, she wouldn't let go of them.

My sister and I knew it was only a matter of time before she switched and so we told the kids and her that we were going. She carried on hugging them. My youngest said, 'Don't be tight mum. She wants us to stay.' I said we would come back another time. We never did.

In the following March of 2015 while I was holding the dying hand of my eighty-three-year-old, my fifty-eight-year-old mother managed to drink herself to death and die alone. Words can't describe what a cruel joke that felt, because if I'd have had the choice of whose hand to have held, in their last moments, then it would have been hers, the one who wanted love and demanded it in the most unloving ways.

My sister gives me a letter. She said she hadn't given it to me before because she thought it may have been another poisoned one. Well, it turned out to be a nice one finally.

Dear Anthea,

I just want to say to you how sorry I am for the last time I saw you. My behavior is out of order. I don't blame you for not wanting to see me again. I feel ashamed of myself. You are my first born and that is special to any mum. I wish I could put the clock back start all over again. You have given me many chances and because of alcohol I threw it back in your face. I don't deserve your forgiveness.

I am very proud of you. You're a great mum to your kids. I know they love you very much.

Anthea, I tried my best but because of depression, I drove you all away from me. I need you very much. please forgive me.

Love mum xx

So, at the funeral for her eulogy I answered her letter.

Dear Mum,

Life was hard for you and in turn at times hard for those who were in your life. There is no question raising your siblings and then raising your children singlehanded was a difficult undertaking. But you raised four intelligent children and with us all having different fathers, that intelligence, genetically speaking could have only come from you.

But mum, your four children suffered as you suffered. No child wants for their mother to feel pain and hurt as often as you did. You battled with depression and didn't win but as your intelligent babes we worked out all the silent, 'I love yous'. It was these things in no particular order.

1) Managing to withstand our little hands stroking your prickly legs when we curled up behind you on the couch.
2) The egg and homemade chips you made when we were upset that Malina would cheekily request could she have chips with the oil.
3) The roast chicken dinner every Sunday back in the day, courtesy of a hard slog with a shopping trolley to Kwik Save. These dinners always resulted with me winding everyone up for a laugh then you would affectionately call me and Lela a pair of daft sods and tell us to go home.
4) Always keeping the house clean and tidy when we were little and the food cupboard full.
5) If our clothes were ever secondhand then our socks were brand new and had to be the whitest of the white.
6) Letting us stay up a bit later on a Thursday to watch Top of the Pops and EastEnders.
7) Getting us used to not having sugar in our tea because we always ran out.

8) Teaching us to stick up for ourselves and to look after people less fortunate than us.
9) Being proud of us for all being brought up in Rusholme and Moss Side and getting ourselves through university.
10) Marrying Patrick and giving us our brother Stefan.

A big gamble four cesareans. But physical pain never fazed you, only heartache. To finish, you bravely fought cancer for which I salute you. The other battles were just too much but in response to your letter, yes mum I do forgive you and yes you are loved. Please rest well and in the meantime, we'll continue to look after each other. You deserve the peace. Goodnight, God Bless.

Your eldest,

Anthea

Coming Home

My Soul Mate Carmen

Getting ready for LB coming home. So he had a weekend at home then back to Strangeways for a week, then home for good, 'Never going back inside again.' Let's see, how things are going to be, the normal everyday things, schoolwork. We have to live and I've got used to the money, full cupboards. Doing the house up, the kids never going without. Not that they ever did, but there have been times when we have been careful with money and watched the pennies as they say. He's home, the kids are happy. Well, bam! A few weeks in and life starts to change. A friend from the past pops up. I've not seen this guy since before LB went away. 'I'm off to watch football, I'm meeting T.' This went on for a while. What I noticed was that T never came to the house. About this time Joan started calling the house. So, a time begins like life before prison. What do I do, what do I do? LB wants to see his son and his son wants to see his dad. LB goes to Joan's house in my head. Is he and her going to take up where they left off? Start an affair again? The first time his son K came to the house it was a Sunday, well me and the kids were in for a shock, as the front door opened, in walks LB, K and his sister. That wasn't the arrangement. Why is she here? The mum said that if the daughter couldn't come then K couldn't either. In the meantime, LB is still meeting T. I'm feeling very uneasy and rightly so. He's up to his old habits he's seeing T's sister. He stayed out late one night till the early hours. I'm ready for him, no more, time to go, no excuses, not going back to that life, pack your bags and go. You know it won't happen again. It's done he says. In the meantime, the kids are still coming here at the weekends. I didn't know how this was affecting our kids. I later found out that our kids (well two of them) would tell K's sister that LB wasn't her dad, so don't call him dad and sometimes they gave her a hard time. She would draw pictures of her, her mum and brother and LB as a family. Still there was the other situation, the final straw. We were packing to go away for the weekend in Birmingham for a friend's party. As we were packing the car, a delivery from a florist arrived, not for me, for LB from T's sister. I went berserk, kicking off at him. The shock on his face. He tells me it was over and this was her not wanting it to be over. She was willing to be the other woman, she wanted him to tell me it was over. We went away for the weekend; it was marred, I couldn't get the incident out of my head. I knew I wasn't going to put up with shit. When we came home, I told him to sort it out or I will. We never heard from her again. Her brother tried to get in touch a few times. LB spoke to him and we haven't heard from him since.

My soul mate LB. How do we know what a soul mate is or means? We hear this saying. Is it your best lover? Best friend? That you would share everything with, your secrets, if you have any, your dreams. I don't know if for some people you know straight away when you meet. LB and I met when we were seven and nine years of age. His family moved a few doors from where we lived. First connection. Our friendship was formed as was our lives only we didn't know it then. We connect in our late teens. It is like we have never been apart, only this time there is a spark there, a flutter in my stomach, a happiness for me, an excitement, a sexual chemistry, a feeling of wanting to be together. All the time impossible in our world and the life we lived at the time.

Soul Mate = someone who understands you. You understand them, you don't always agree with each other. But you respect each other.

Honesty = wow we had to work on that because of our lifestyles we lived by, we are honest with each other.

Trust = has many meanings, to be faithful, as in making decisions, discussing things together.

LOVE = being in love, physical love, and caring. Side by side fighting for what we want together, the disbelievers and negative vibes. Being ourselves. No pretence, side by side like an army. As we have grown older, we are settled with each other, comfortable. Each other knowing what we want from life and each other, still having our friends and doing our pastimes and hobbies, but knowing we are best friends. Encouraging each other. Feeling each other's pain. Sharing with each other. Picking each other up when we are falling down. We can still have an argument, a discussion and be friends. I'm the one who will not speak or keep silent. I've had to work on my feelings, LB is very laid back.

Is that a soul mate? Our Passion is still there.

What Did My Mum Want From Me

Tia

What the fuck did my mum want from me? It really did fluctuate from the impossible to the most simplistic. I knew she wanted the best for me but even that was questionable by the way she went about things. She'd show off a good School Report to people around her, but I don't remember her sitting down writing or drawing with us. However, she did every time she got her Monday book, AKA benefit money, she'd buy me and my sister a notebook. I suppose there was encouragement there on some level to be academic. She never did it often but whenever she could afford it, she'd let us buy a book from the school book club. This probably happened a couple of times a year and we treasured those books.

Oh, but let's not forget the paedophile that lived across the road that I sat for hours and hours with looking through books and talking about history and science. When she told me he was a paedo as an adult, I was like, 'What the actual fuck!! Why did you let me spend so much time with him?' Her response was, there was nothing to worry about because, 'He liked boys.' Eye roll; I despair. I really can't fathom what she was thinking, but admittedly I hate to say aloud, I learned so much from that man. Kevin, he was called. He was white with a massive, long nose, hunched shoulders, and he lived on a diet of biscuits, tea and fags. He always had a cig, puffing on it from the corner of his mouth, while he told me lots of stuff. Back then in the 80s we didn't think there was anything wrong with puffing away and blowing carbon monoxide and nicotine all over kids. He did teach me that girls could car mind when City were playing a match at Maine Rd. I tried it. And I did well. I told the football fans, 'Can I mind your car please Sir and I will actually mind it because I live here on the street and those lads don't hang around as soon as you pay them. In fact, you can pay half now and half when you see me sat here on the curb on your return.' I had business patter, age nine. I got away with car minding for a good few Saturdays until my mum found out and went mental. She said it was begging. I wasn't allowed to go trick or treating either she said that was begging too. She said a weirdo could kidnap me and do weird stuff. The irony. I told Kevin and he said, stick to reading and he gave me this massive, big black book. It was a hardback with gold and silver writing, and it was all about the Victorians. I think it was a really good quality book and really old. He told me to look after it and to be careful as it was worth a bit of money. I made the mistake of taking it to my nana and granddad's and it never came back home with me. My mum said my granddad probably nicked it to sell down the pub for the price of a pint. I was hurt and disappointed, but I didn't say anything 'cause I was that quiet kid taking it all in.

My mom had been out the night before and was really hungover. I was chattering away telling her that the cat, Leo, fell off the gate, but he had managed to scramble back up and it was really funny. While I was telling her, she slipped and fell down the whole twelve steps of the stairs. She landed on top of my poor little sister. My mum was on the hippo side of big and my sister was a lanky but skinny little thing. My eyes widened and I shouted, 'Lela are you OK?' I asked my sister this because I figured she would be the injured party. My mum went absolutely apeshit. She said it was my fault for, 'Wittering on about a cat falling off a gate first thing in the fucking morning!' I said nothing out loud but inwardly I was thinking, 'It's because you're a fat cow who drinks too much!'

We laughed about it years later, about her falling on top of poor Lela at the bottom of the stairs of Newport St. It's strange how many of us laugh about things that at the time were far from funny and yet later we laugh hard about them. It's probably how we've survived.

I've been thinking a lot about having a white mum and a black father, lately. Especially since we have seen a seismic eruption of the world and Black Lives Matter protests. I'm questioning would she be surprised by it all if she was alive today?

I left my house this morning to quietly go and weed out my allotment and then just like that, I got off and joined a Black Lives Matter protest in the city center to scream my lungs out and have everyone around me echo the words, 'I can't breathe.' For a moment it brings me back to a few memories of being close to my mum when I was really little. About three maybe four, I was sat on the arm of a chair while she sat in the chair and I played with her thick black shiny hair. I told her that she looks after me and then when I'm big she will become a child and I will become a mum. Oh my God, that kind of already happened. She said, 'No you'll get big and you'll become a woman and a mum to your own child and then I get to be old and you look after me.' The sad part is she didn't actually get to be old because of drinking, she drank herself to death years later. She told me what racism was. She tried to explain it the best she could. She said it was when white people didn't like black or brown people without a reason. I said but why do they have to hate if they don't have a reason? She said racism will always exist. My heart sunk. I think she saw it in my eyes. She then said, I don't think racism will disappear in my lifetime, but it will do in yours. I see now she knew she was lying, but sometimes those types of lies told to your children are acceptable.

Watching the news over the last week, it's been moving/ emotional to see the world awaken and its attempt to end injustices. Palestinians and Israelis have even protested Black Lives Matter together. Young, white Australians have stood next to their country's indigenous aboriginal people shoulder-to-shoulder and proclaimed Black Lives Matter. Even here in Manchester the white population outnumbered the black in a crowd of around twenty thousand people and they also screamed Black Lives Matter. I kind of personally needed white people to scream it louder. After all it wasn't black people that invented racism so therefore, we shouldn't be the ones having to search for the solution. In this moment I'm thinking maybe my mum didn't lie to me as a small child when she said racism would end in my lifetime but then I open Facebook and there they are, the ones that don't get it, the ones who proclaim, 'I'm not racist but.' And then there are the so called friends that are more outraged that a building or a statue of a slave trader or monument is being defaced or destroyed. None of those people shared the same outrage for the eight minutes forty-six seconds of a white police officer kneeling on a black man's neck, calling for his mother. Calling for his fucking mother. I couldn't bring myself to watch this public execution that seemed to spread like wildfire through social media and made it to mainstream media in the comfort of our homes. If truth be known I don't know what it would do to me or what I would do if I watched it all while I am feeling the way I am. But I have read the words in articles of what he said. Knowing he called for his mother was like he knew he was going to die, and it absolutely hurts my whole being as I envisaged what I would do if that was my own son.

I have so many questions for myself to face after lockdown is over. I'm not concerned in going back to the nine – five modern day slavery with a white boss who told me off for arguing with a racist. I've always had a mouth. I've always stood up for what was wrong in the world. My mother had a mouth too. She always fought for the vulnerable and championed the underdog and I have done the same time and time again. I can't deny sometimes, I want my crazy mother alive to tell me what to do, and what not to do. I want my black community to do what the Jewish and Asian communities do and somehow keep the pound for as long as it can in the community; pass sixteen hands before it passes out. I want us to be more inclined to buy books or make long-term investments for our children rather than skint ourselves to find the latest pair of trainers or new gaming console. I think my white mum wouldn't want me being so insular and would rather me be more outward with love and be all embracing. I have always been those things but the anger and the hurt that is dwelling inside me makes me think the way I am thinking. If my mum were to disapprove, I would have to say to her the only mistake we people of colour made was believing that just because our ancestors built the empire, wore the same clothes, shared the same language and practiced the same religion, we mistakenly thought we were somehow equal to white people and they would see us so. We own nothing but our skin. Maybe that's why they think our lives are so worthless and disposable, maybe that's why they can watch us be executed on a TV and be more upset by a building being destroyed.

I'm grown enough now to know anger and watching the likes of Tommy fuckin' Robinson supporters chant monkey noises and telling us to go back home is another assault on my already damaged soul and mind. I'm working hard to shut that noise out, to focus and channel my energy into bigger and more positive things and I hold on to all my mother figures I have in my life; both black and white, they are pulling me through another shitstorm in this thing we call life.

The Wedding Days

Catherine

It is a cold January morning; I cannot member the date. I have booked a cab for 9:00am. Do not even remember what day it was. I get up quite early have a quick shower, cream suit on, rust colour blouse and boots. Went downstairs. Was not expecting to see anyone, suddenly I heard my sister's voice, 'Where are you going?' I look shocked, she answered for me, 'You are going to get married, aren't you?' I laughed said nothing and left the house.

In the cab on my way to Salford Registry Office. It's freezing that morning there is frost on the ground. As I arrive at the registry office, I can see Mr Proctor with two people who I don't recognise. I was introduced to them as Jack and Maureen, they were going to be our witnesses. I was not aware we needed them. Anyway, I took no notice of them or why they needed to be there. We walked into the registry building and stood in the foyer waiting for our names to be called.

Here I am standing with two strangers and Mr Proctor whom I hardly knew, I'm looking at them, crapping myself, I go to the loo. Mr Proctor said hurry up I think it is us next. I already started to hate him, for what happened to my son.

Once in the loo I start to panic. There was a small window which I opened firstly to get some air then I decided to climb out. Suddenly I find myself in the middle of a busy roundabout in the centre of Salford but free from the pending gloom. A cab pulls up tells me to get in. He is asking me questions, I don't answer, just give him my mum's address. When I got to mum's

I went back to bed, I never told anyone what I'd done, and laughed at the thought of those three standing there waiting for me to come back. I cannot remember if Mr Proctor called me that day, I just got on with my incredibly stressful sad life – living in misery without my son, with my mum and my two brothers.

Some weeks later I heard that Mr Proctor had gone back to sea, so I was surprised to receive a phone call from him in February. He was in Romania and told me his father had died and he was coming back to the UK for the funeral. I have received a job offer from the GPO (General Post Office) where I wanted to be a telephone operator, however they offered me a job as a telegraphist. I wasn't really interested in any type of work but needed to get out of the house for my sanity, as I am just drifting full of confusion and sadness.

Mr Proctor comes back, the funeral is over, he calls and asks if we could meet? I met him as the alternative was another miserable night at home. He asked why I did what I did, but he also thought it was funny, he said he admired me for that. Then he tells me he will be going back to sea shortly. We meet a few more times when he suggested I go away with him. For me to do this we would have to be married. Looking at my options I thought fuck it! I can do this I will escape the pain and misery and runaway from all that happened.

March 9th 1979 same rules as before, same outfit, cab ordered, no sister this time and we had a wedding ring, not sure what we were going to use the first time round probably would have borrowed one. I'm in the cab, the weather's better than last time.

I arrive at the registry office, Mr Proctor, Jack and Maureen are already waiting. I look at them start to feel queasy, might get diarrhoea, need a drink! We are standing waiting not saying a word, not even looking at each other.

Jack told me later he was terrified that I might do the same thing again.

Our names are called, and we make it to the room. Everything is going smoothly until it's my turn to say my vows, I start to laugh, the more I tried to stop, the more uncontrollable the laugh becomes, my stomach is hurting I am doubled over laughing. I couldn't contain myself, just laughing louder and louder and louder. I could not see anything in the room, just remember Mr Proctor standing next to me, I can hear the registrar telling me she understands people do get nervous, but I need to pull myself together as there were other people waiting outside. Finally, I managed to stop, said my vows. We left the registry office. And headed straight to the pub. I do believe it was about 10:30 in the morning when we arrived at the pub which never closed. I ordered a huge rum and black, a legacy from my Reno days.

I drink myself into oblivion, with Proctor, Jack and Maureen. We didn't talk much. I remember Mr Proctor saying he was going to look after me, I should put my past behind me now. That was like a knife stabbing my heart. I hated him at that moment, and I hated myself for what I had done and what I'd let happen to my son.

I kept seeing a guy on the other side of the bar, he's looking over at us. I thought that could be Mr Proctor with red hair, and Proctor's was black. I found out that they were brothers and they never spoke to each other; I should have known what a cold calculating pig Proctor was then. I do believe they both shared the same woman for a time. She was now his brother's wife.

We didn't eat at all that day and it's 8:30 in the evening I walked out of the pub grab a cab arrive at mum's house absolutely smashed. Mum and brother sat on the sofa and I tripped up. I said to mum, 'I've done something awful.' Without saying another word mum shouts, 'You got married!!! I'll kill him.'

I throw the marriage certificate at her and run upstairs, mum came after me. I jumped into my brother's bed. She's hitting me, and shouting at me, 'You're not married to that bastard!' I am under the covers hoping it will stop soon, my brother is downstairs shouting me, he's telling me Proctor is on the phone. Mum runs down, 'I'll fecking give you he's on the phone!' She grabs the phone from my brother and screams at Proctor, 'Don't you come to my house you feckin bastard!!' (He is eighteen years older than me.) She puts the phone down, all goes quiet in the house and we go to bed.

I didn't hear from Proctor for nine days. I'm still living at mum's, never bothered with the job offer, I'm in an even bigger mess now.

Proctor calls me one evening. 'What's going on?' He said, 'We need to sort this.' He suggests mum, him and I go out for dinner, now that was a mistake.

Mum agreed and we get a cab to Rusholme. We went to an Indian Restaurant. Mum and I met Proctor at the restaurant we had a small amount of food and I was drinking as I was nervous. Proctor pays the bill, and we go to the Red Lion in Withington for a drink.

Proctor becomes more confident with drink, he asks my mum about my dad this was not a good topic, as I was not even sure my dad was the man mum said he was. Mum admits she wishes she were still with him. I can hear the shit they are talking. But as usual I'm not taking a lot of notice. Just listening to the music on the jukebox – Rose Royce *Love Don't Live Here Anymore* is playing, it was a big tune that year, always made me cry. I just drank more, to numb the pain; my son didn't live here anymore. I completely disconnected myself from everything and everyone around me.

It is getting late. We leave the Red and have a quick drink in the Cotton Tree which is on the way back to mum's. Mum and I are tired, so we tell Proctor we are going home, he is talking to the landlord and says he will finish his drink and follow on. It is about 10:30pm; by 12:30am Proctor had not arrived back; mum and I went to bed, and mum made sure all the doors were locked.

2:00am – My brother shouts, 'Mum there's someone at my window.'

'Shut up!' Shouts mum.

My brother calls again, 'Mum! There's someone at the window and they are tapping.' (Paul's bedroom is upstairs.)

Mum shouts, 'Stop being stupid Paul and go to sleep.'

'Mum they are banging on the window now. They are on my windowsill. Please MUM!!!'

I hear all this but I'm half asleep, I've had one too many drinks so not totally compos mentis, then the shit hits the fan. I hear mum: 'Feck! That bastard.' Mum jumps out of bed, pink winceyette nighty, fluffy dressing gown, no teeth. 'I'll feckin' kill him. The bastard! Coming here at this time.'

I realise Proctor is on the windowsill. I better get up, mum rushes past me, and pushes me aside, she runs down the stairs, like a mad woman, into the back garden where she gets the prop for the washing line, runs back to the front of the house, sees Proctor who has managed to climb the drainpipe, and is holding on by the skin of his teeth to the window frame of my brother's bedroom.

I am standing at the front door dazed.

Mum flies around the corner to get the washing line prop. 'Get down you bastard!' She shouts, as she swings the prop across the window causing him to shake, she did this twice, before he loses his balance and fell to the ground. He is lying in the garden now, mum gives him a kick, tells me to get inside. Jeeze! I just did as I was told, leaving Proctor lying in the garden, not knowing whether he was even able to move.

Next day Proctor has gone. Mum's new boyfriend arrives, awful guy I could not stand him. White hair, red face, looked like a skinned pig. He was racist. A nasty man. Proctor calls, tells me he is going to LA in a couple of days. 'If you want to come with me you will need to meet me tonight as we have to go to the American Embassy in the morning to get your visa.'

He will not be waiting around, lol, I think he was at the end of his tether.

What do I do? I pack my bag, Proctor is calling, my brother is begging me not to go, I feel sick. I love my brother, but I had to escape from the pain and misery of losing my son. There's so much noise, Proctor still calling, my brother begging.

For fuck sake I am twenty years old, I cannot cope any longer. A cab pulls up with my mum's other partner, he is very upset, he has just seen mum at work with the vile new guy. Mum ended her relationship with Rene who was an engineer in the Danish Merchant Navy. He had been coming round for a few years now, I liked him, he was funny, and somehow gave the impression he cared. He picked up his belongings, and told me I should go with Proctor, get away for a while, we shared a cab back to Manchester him crying, I told him he is better off without her.

Mr Proctor was waiting for me at the train station, we travelled first class to London. We would have been flying only all internal flights were on strike. I had no idea what that meant. I thought internal was something that you had when you had a baby.

We stayed at the Park Lane Hotel I ate lemon sole for the first time in my life. Next day we had priority access to the American Embassy. We got my visa and went directly to Heathrow Airport and there the adventure began.

The Maiden Voyage

Catherine

I'm on my way to San Fran – little old me, I've never been on a plane before, Proctor spends most of his time at the back of the plane (you could smoke in those days), I was just fascinated with the in-house entertainment. We travelled business class – food comes around all the time, drink as much as you like, all served on proper plates and with proper glasses. Of course I had a few too many drinks.

We arrived at San Fran where we are catching a flight to LA however we were delayed at Heathrow so we miss the flight. Proctor is arguing with security trying to get us through to catch the next flight. That didn't happen so we stayed at an airport hotel, where I had a huge pizza – another new experience. The next day Proctor took me to Fisherman's Wharf where we had crab? Crab! I didn't even know people ate that. We are sitting at a large wooden table. The crabs come in a basket with wood mallets for us to beat the crabs and eat the meat, (they are dead). What an experience! I loved the crab meat. We were sat by the sea and could see Alcatraz on the rock. Little old me living it up.

We finally get a flight to LA and arrive at the ship. It is like a floating hotel. I am like a child; I have no idea a ship this size exists. It's roasting in LA when I left the UK it was cold and windy; I do not have any summer clothes – Mr Proctor gives me some dollars!! Loads of them and arranges a lift into town for me. I go shopping in LA. I just walk by all the stores staring, looking. What shall I buy? Where should I buy? I found a large department store, walked in. The assistants are looking, (probably thought I was a shop lifter).

One approaches me, I tell her I am on a ship, I am from England, OMG they love Brits – and happily show me how to spend my $. Bikinis, shorts, t-shirts, denims, undies and a few smart bits for dinner on the ship. That is it. I am done! No money left, I meet the agent who brought me to town he takes me back to the ship.

There is a very grand ship birthed next to us that was none other than the 'Queen Mary' restored to her former glory. Not that I knew anything about it.

Back on the ship I am greeted by the steward who looks after my accommodation – cabin. He takes me there. Once in the room, Proctor comes up – he is happy that I am happy with all my new purchase – I mean WTF one day I'm in Withington depressed, three days later I'm on board a huge vessel in LA this can't be real. Proctor changes into his Whites (uniform). I get ready and we go to the bar, where I met all the other officers including two cadets – Alan and Ozzy who were my age, everyone else was much older. We have drinks then the steward comes to the bar to let us know dinner is served. We all walk to the dining room it's white tablecloths and silver service. The only time I saw this was when I was scrubbing pans in Chorlton Golf Club – and now I'm the one being served. WTF I think I was a little uncomfortable with this, still a few drinks sorted that out.

Another wife joined the next day, her name was Moira she was married to one of the engineers, much older than me and had travelled a lot. Before we set sail we were invited onto the Queen Mary for drinks with the captain. Unfortunately we were sailing that evening, so it was all hands on deck. We sailed from LA to Singapore. Moira and I sat by the pool, the sun was blazing, we were in the middle of the ocean with no shade. Moira did not use sunscreen. That evening we had a dinner dance on board, she did not join us, as she was severely burnt. I did not see her for days – when she re-appeared, she had loose skin from the burst blisters, it was awful, she got into the pool and the skin started shredding. I have never seen anything like it. Layers of skin floating on the surface of the pool, I think I will be sick. I find a steward and ask him to empty the pool.

Life was very quiet in the daytime so I started reading, novels: *The Drifters, Chesapeake, The World According to Garp,* then Malcom X, Martin Luther King, all kind of black rights and civil movement books, along with an endless stream of US radio stations playing soul music. I am learning a lot.

Singapore was amazing. We went to Change Alley where everything was genuine fake – I bought Levi jeans. Later we went to Raffles Hotel, sat there having cocktails, I had a pina colada it was sweet so I could drink a few. Singapore is known as the garden city, Proctor knew it well so he took me everywhere. We had a great time. He bought me a genuine watch with a big brand name at the time maybe 'Omega'??

I am becoming accustomed to this life and have adapted well to the stewards, doing everything for me. I try not to think of home – of my brother and my son. We continue to go fishing for lobster-clams-crabs-crayfish, massive prawns. There was always a large fruit platter in the officers' mess. Food was amazing: kedgeree for breakfast, nasi goreng for Sunday lunch.

I would play monopoly with the cadets it could get quite heated, sometimes one game went on for days. I did start to see Proctor's jealous side; he would insist we went to our room early in the evening, would bring his beer and suggest I had had enough to drink. Still I cracked on – the Captain taught me how to play chess, all in all I was growing as a person.

From Singapore we went to Korea. The sea was rough, it went cold, there was not much to do, we were sailing for weeks. Once we arrived in Korea it was cold and damp, but I was getting off that ship! Moira came with me – the agent took us into town and left us there. No one spoke English.

There were open sewers on the streets, and people keep stopping and staring at us. We walked around the town, but Moira got scared we couldn't find where the agent had dropped us. I suggested we get on a bus. They will know the docks. She is crying now, at forty-three years well-travelled I am shocked. She sits on a wall when I see the shit floating by as it's an open sewer. We jump on a bus, everyone stands up, WTF – I try to get some understanding from the driver, making ship noises and arm and hand gestures of a ship sailing. Moira is hiding behind me. Anyway the people on the bus decide we want the docks, they keep touching me – I'm freaked out, Moira is still crying when we finally reach the docks, everyone claps as we get off the bus. I had not realized just how big the docks were, like miles and miles of sea, ships, industrial cranes, and black soot from the coal.

I saw a bar, we went in, I order a beer for both of us, and just sat there, men kept coming over showing me wads of money? Confused? I order more drinks I point to what looked like gin. It is madness, there is a line of men all showing me money. I am pushing them away – when thankfully Proctor and others from the ship arrive – they have had the word two British women are in the brothel on the quayside. Ha ha. I could have made a fortune. Moira was never allowed to come out with me after that (ironic).

Leaving Korea with a cargo of coal destined for Canada which was a long cold passage, Moira didn't leave her room much. Cadets and I continued playing monopoly and other board games, along with drinking a lot – I read in the day and started noticing my knickers were going missing from the drying room, which was mine and Proctor's. I had drawn the line at the stewards doing our washing – I kept quiet about the knickers. Thought it was my imagination.

We arrive in Vancouver. I wanted to learn to Ski. Proctor booked lessons on the Grouse Mountain, this was hilarious – I never passed the kids' slope. Proctor was on the cable cars going to the top – he did not realise till it was too late, however he managed to ski all the way down. The kids would see me on the rope that pulled you up, they would be shouting, 'English lady jump!' They knew I would be flying off at some point. We spent six weeks in Canada. It was marvellous. Proctor took me out most nights and we met lovely people. Before we left Canada, I bought new knickers.

From Canada we go to Indonesia, then the Cayman Islands where we order chicken and rice. The bartender got a chicken from the garden and broke its neck, then cooked it. I saw pink flamingos walking in the clear blue sea. One of the cadets ran away with a prostitute. Once found, he had to be locked in his cabin until we sailed.

We continued crab and lobster fishing when we were inland – my knickers continued to go missing – and I finally told Proctor who was not happy. He blamed the stewards who were Hong Kong Chinese, didn't speak much English and were away from home eleven months of the year. Of course Proctor decides to tell everyone on board. I am fucking embarrassed. The Captain says there will be an enquiry, now everyone is looking for the missing knickers (how embarrassing), the poor Stewards getting a really hard time from Proctor.

One day one of the stewards saw the cadet leave our drying room, he told the captain – who had the cadet's room searched, where they found all my washed knickers. I think it started as a joke but got out of hand. Now I am not allowed to talk to Ozzy and he is too embarrassed to look at me, we were good companions. Alan had been confined to his room when we got to port. The captain could not risk him running away with another prostitute, as he was only seventeen.

Back in the USA we are in Philadelphia, the Philly sound blasting on the radio – McFadden and Whitehead was a big tune (*Ain't No Stopping Us Now*), it was all black music, soul, as much as you like, I love it.

Proctor takes the day off and we get on – YES! a greyhound bus, to New York. New York – I can't believe my ears – OMG I've seen it in the movies – *Shaft*, *Hill Street Blues*, that's where I'm going, Music, Music, Music all the way – Proctor knows NY better than Manchester, he takes me to all the sites, Empire State, Twin Towers, Central Park, Grand Central Station, Broadway too many to mention. We ate hot clams and drank whisky. Later I had clam chowder – a New York Strip (steak), we spent the whole day and night there, I bought pictures, music, more denim. I was speechless the whole time, how was this happening to little old me from Chorlton-on-Medlock, well it is! And I am taking it.

On the Bus back to Philly, it was early hours of the morning when we arrived. I was laden with bags, and very tired.

We were circled by a group of young men, they just started walking around us – I was scared, Proctor told me to stand still he said to the guys, 'Piss off we want to pass.' I shit myself Proctor stood his ground, grabbed me and said, 'Let's go.' A guy approached Proctor, he told him to 'Piss off.' He told them all to, 'Piss off.' I see Proctor's Salford street roots coming out, scared of no fucker. Lucky a taxi pulled up and a police car, we got into the taxi. I wanted to cry.

Next day we go into Philadelphia, walking and looking happy, Proctor was with me, some guy asked if I had a price? I was not sure what he meant then I saw Proctor punch him to the ground. We just walked on. 'Jeeze!' We went to a bar where we could not get served as I didn't have my passport, and the bartender thought I was Proctor's daughter. Hehehe.

From Philly we went to Baltimore, I realised I love the East Coast of America, a bit of danger, a lot of excitement, music and characters.

Sheltering from the rain a guy comes over, 'Where you from man?'

I say 'England.'

'Oh! Paris, England. I've been there,' was his reply, before he asks me to hit him with a dollar. I hit him with five.

We've been away for six months – Proctor wanted to go back to the UK, his trips were usually four months, but his replacement didn't turn up in the States, so he had to stay on board.

We are heading to Europe – 'Yugoslavia', I think the voyage was ten days. When we arrive, I found out we were not birthing just picking up Proctor's and two other officers' replacements. A small tugboat came alongside the ship.

It was pitch black and we were in the middle of the sea – a rope ladder was hung down the side of the ship. Which was half a mile out of the water. We had to climb over the side of the ship onto the rope ladder, and walk down it, then wait for a wave to lift the tugboat out of the water, so you could jump onto the tug. I was crying – I am not great with heights or the dark, and I can hardly swim, so all my worst nightmares are here with me.

"I can't do this," I told Proctor, but he has gone, the engineer has gone, and the electrician has gone all new crew are on board – the captain is telling me he has to sail, Proctor is shouting come on, I am crying – really crying, I cannot move I am frozen, and Proctor has left me alone.

Eventually the captain says he will have to sail (because of the tide) they are going back to the States, I can go with them, and fly home from there. The electrician came back up, he and the captain help me, the electrician climbed over the side the captain held me until the electrician was safe on the ladder then the captain let me go, the electrician went down each step, then me, I was almost sat on his head. We are at the end now and he jumps! 'Fucking hell!' I am terrified standing on the last rung of the ladder, with nothing but the sea underneath me, terrified to jump. This is a living nightmare. I missed the wave and jumped as the tug was going back down, I could have broken my back. I didn't speak to Proctor; another one of those times when I hated him. We were taken to the hotel, I drank and went to bed. We slept in separate beds. We were supposed to be flying back to the UK two days later, but there was disruption with air traffic control, so we ended up spending four weeks in Yugoslavia. Such a beautiful country, wonderful scenery.

I ate Caviar. We drove through the Alps to Milan – where we finally got a flight to the UK.

We had been away for seven and a half months – I was completely brown from the sun, my hair was wild, and blonder than it had ever been – I had put weight on, and we had nowhere to live. My Mum said we could stay at hers.

I had bought loads of presents for the family, was so happy to see my brother Douglas. We played baseball in the park. I got a haircut, and for the first time I realized I had changed color – we started to look for a house. Which brought us to Marple.

The Walking Stick

How I Feel Now
Carmen

When you see a person using a walking stick you think they have had an accident or they are old. Well LB was neither: he had a stroke. Well, he actually had a TIA a mini stroke. This lasted twenty-four hours. Doctors said it's a warning of sorts, you can have a full stroke. Very scary for the person concerned. You can lose the use of arms, legs, or your speech. This happened in the early part of 2002, February. Then four weeks later, I was out shopping with one of our daughters in Stockport on our way home in teatime traffic, when my mobile phone rings, it's our son-in-law, he says LB is not well but he doesn't know what's wrong with him or what to do. You know when you know something is really wrong that's the feeling I had. We got home. As soon as I looked at LB, I knew something was wrong. He couldn't speak properly, the left side of his body was not working, he couldn't walk, his arm and leg wouldn't coordinate. He thought he was making sense when he wasn't. Our daughter went into nurse mode, (she is a brilliant nurse by profession) called the emergency services, took control. Our poor son-in-law was as pale as a ghost. I was trying to be calm, inside I was a bundle of nerves. I kept asking him if he was OK, trying to get him to speak. Asking questions which he couldn't answer. Eventually the ambulance arrives. Great paramedics do all their tests and say we need to get him to hospital. I go in the ambulance with LB, they put him in a wheelchair, we go to the

MRI hospital, I can see that LB is frightened. When we arrive at the hospital, we are taken straight into the emergency and seen straight away. LB is admitted and kept in for two weeks. Has lots of tests to see if they can find out what caused the stroke? He had physio to help him regain the use of his left leg and arm. He made real progress, gained his speech daily. The doctors couldn't explain what caused the stroke. So, he was sent home. We had to make adjustments to our home. Before coming home, LB had to be able to walk up a flight of stairs, feed himself which he did with great determination. Once your home you're left on your own, so now the hard work begins. Chasing up the physio appointments to come to the house. Extra help, as in money as I couldn't go to work, having to ask family to help. Mood swings, depression setting in, he slept a lot, being home, made LB feel safer, but for me it was a time of worry, wondering if he was going to have another stroke. The fear of not knowing if I/we could cope. I was LB's carer now. It was a slow recovery, washing and dressing him. I always seemed to be asking, 'Are you alright?' He said stop asking me, when I'm not OK, I'll let you know. It was a slow recovery, learning to walk, dress yourself, simple things like using the stairs, using the shower. The physio helped LB a lot; he is a very strong willed and determined man. I had to learn patience and understanding. It took months for me to feel I could relax and leave him in the house on his own. To watch the person, you love and care about, not be able to do the simplest of things is heart breaking. Wondering if they will ever be themselves again. But he did, started walking, making a cup of tea, we would do little walks up the street. He made a full recovery, went back to work. Social life back on track. Everything was great. Bang on ten years later, we are at home in the lounge, LB says to me it's happening again. I say what is? But I think I know, yes, it's another stroke. I call 999, get through to the emergency services a lovely lady very calm, she's asking me lots of questions, can he swallow, what's his breathing like? An ambulance arrives;

we are taken to Salford Royal Hospital. Apparently, it's one of the best hospitals for head and brain injuries. I called the kids to let them know where we were and what had happened. Ten minutes after us getting to the hospital our daughter the nurse arrives as we are being rushed into cubicle and a doctor arrives does his examination. We are taken up to another floor, where this doctor says to save LB life and hopefully stop him having another stroke, he wants to do a procedure on LB where they give you an injection and the next twenty-four hours are crucial. I didn't know what to do for the best, I remember saying I wanted to ask my daughter her advice. He said we didn't have time for that and started running along this corridor, pushing the trolley that LB was on. By the time our daughter had found us and was running with us, she said she had never seen a consultant or doctor run with a patient in all her years of nursing. They got him to the theatre, did the procedure, it saved his life. He was in Salford Royal for three weeks, then in the MRI hospital for about another three weeks and so rehabilitation starts all over again. This time more intense. Black moods, shouting at each other, but not for long. We learn to adjust. Things have to be put in place at home. To help LB's recovery: grab rails at the front and back door, in the bathroom to help him get in and out of the bath and shower, the front doorstep had to be raised. Special feet on the bottom of the sofa that he sat on. Medication had to be adjusted and changed. I was his carer again. This time I knew I had to ask for help, financial and getting the right help for LB. I had to keep phoning about his home physio and benefits as we didn't think LB would work again. Which he hasn't. By the time he had finished his physio at the hospital and at home he was walking but his left leg dragged. In comes the walking stick – NHS grey metal one (I've since bought him a couple of nice ones).

I Have Missed My Soul

Tia

I have missed my soul, just to be silent and still; feel my breath, my pumping heart and connect my mind back with my soul. It's been a peaceful reminder I am healing. How many of us confine our souls to a boxed cage, where knobs and undesirables slip in and out of the bars taking a piece of you, and with it your peace? I think many of us do. We don't want them to but our capacity to adamantly put our foot down to stop it is blocked because so many knobs are bleeding clever; emotional assassins that manage to start some small shit that isn't even big enough to mention or challenge. I could pack all my attributes and flaws into neat little boxes, and perfectly place them to make a neat, rectangular wall and then I could choose to make that rectangle into a sturdy brick wall and hope it lasts an eternity. That wall, of my strengths and weaknesses, could only last a lifetime, not an eternity and it's soulless.

I feel like everyone else in the modern world has also been placing bricks. I've been building a wall for protection and recently I've been pulling that wall down, hoping I'll connect and find life, a soul there. A soul can't live in a hard place. I have to take a pickaxe to the bricks and mortar. Destruction isn't always a bad thing. Sometimes it's the life declutter you need. I've done the physically destructive stuff in the past and that shit hurts but it's also the big cry out. Lost. Then I've done the psychological destructive, going too fast, wanting results quick and achieving nothing and getting there fast and wearing myself out in the process.

I did a work personality test the other day. It was better than checking on a Facebook quiz what sort of potato I was or what sort of cat I was in a past life. The personality test said I was the protector. Sounds about right but even though it seems a great quality it's also code for this person can't come in at the bottom end of a company because she'll rattle too many cages. So, after killing myself doing a manual labour job (—yes, because I didn't want the stress of tutoring anymore because I'm a bloody perfectionist who doesn't cut corners but burns out in doing so) I get laid off ... the classic zero hour contract that has helped keep the rich and the poor divide gap strong. Lockdown hits and I've been made redundant and in order to survive I'm going to have to rough it a bit on Universal Credit. I'm not upset, I'm not scared. The whole world looks like it's fallen to shit because of a pandemic and I'm in this realm of calm. The beginning of lockdown, a couple of bars fell from this imprisoned soul of mine that I had forgotten, through neglect. It actually turns out I had been going out to work for roughly an extra £20 a week in comparison to what state benefit had been paying out. And let's just say I probably spent £20 on getting to work and on lunches so in theory I could have stayed at home, looked after my kids full time and not done my own head in listening to bobbins radio stations and mundane conversations about TV programs I hadn't watched. I also wouldn't have had to spend so much time resisting the urge to throat punch colleagues that were being racist and xenophobic. But regret is a terrible thing. I am a half cup full kind of girl and I always take a lesson from every situation whether it's good or bad, that I find myself in. So, take the rat race nine to five out of the equation and I get to do all the stuff that gets overlooked. You know that shit cupboard you've been dying to sort out which holds all that potential useful stuff in, but you've not touched it since you moved into the house. I have about five of those types of cupboards. I've tackled two of them this week. It felt great. Who is this person? I thought. Who has actually given the plates, the bowls, the side plates their own spot and no longer has to clunk about swearing when trying to get one from the bottom of the pile because they were all squashed together in one single pile because of lack of space. Thank you said the bowl, thank you said the side plate... I've not lost it. The plates haven't become my friends, but I forgot about my inner voice and soul that used to sit with me in everything I did. The nine to five can really have you on autopilot. Just an empty vessel of a body doing pointless stuff that gets you numbers in the bank you then flip your plastic on card readers to buy food, clothes, alcohol to then repeat probably until the day you fucking die. Your inner voice not screaming loudly enough, what the fuck are you doing, modern day slave?

My soul has been returning to me and each day she has done something for me. Sometimes my soul slipped out and tapped other people on the shoulder, who then reminded me of stuff. Social media for example, can soon become your new nine to five and take over your Goddamn mind if you let it. Choice has become my new friend, introduced by my soul. Your soul will introduce you to the best if you release those bars. It has the capacity to do that. And every day, sat at the dresser, brushing my hair we discuss inside my head what we are going to do today. In the past I would open mail, glance at mail, decide it wasn't quite recycled material, stuff mail at the side of bookshelf and repeat ten times. After that, I'd have reminders of the same letters, not actioned, then I'd be stressed out by how untidy the shelf is and overwhelmed at which bill or letter should be actioned first. But now I'm like a boss and CEO of my own life. I can't remember the last time I didn't action a piece of mail straight away. Again, who is this person?

I did chuckle to myself when I organized my knicker and sock drawer and I thought, 'Fuckinell, well, you've arrived at middle age.' But I hear there are people half my age that do that sort of thing. It's probably about time I got organized. I think that's where anxiety lives for me, in amongst the clutter and the chaos. I used to read about Feng shui years ago but to put it into practice and bloody benefit from it, was another thing entirely.

Wardrobe next, clothes everywhere. The ones I've not touched in an age, all linked to a job roll or dates that were best left for the confines of a charity bag. I'll put that on today's To Do List. Oh yeah, I'm actually totally done with writing a to do list. They depress me when I'm writing the same shit the next day with all my energies zapped because of lack of completion. It makes me feel a bit of a failure. Now I write an 'I have done list'. It so works for me. I should have done it years ago. So, what else have I decluttered in this freeing of my soul? Ah yes, men! It will come as no surprise that I had three rendezvouses during lockdown. I'll probably wait to write about them post germ World War Three. No drama though and nothing that acquired me getting any more gray hair. That's progress for me. I have missed my soul and she is so glad to have me back.

Beginning Of The End

Catherine

November 1985

Mr Proctor and I had been married for six years we lived in a three-bedroom semi which we bought from new in Marple, Cheshire.

We had two wonderful daughters and Mr Proctor was at sea most of the time. Spending six months away and two months at home. I didn't travel that much with him because the children, needed stability. When he was in Europe the girls and I would go out and join the ship until it sailed. I had made lots of new friends – ladies who had children the same age as mine. I enjoyed being part of the community, taking the kids to ballet, gym, Brownies, swimming, picnics in the park, lunches at pub. Without realising it I had become part of middle-class suburbia and I liked it. We moved from that house to a much larger older property this has great big utility room, a playroom, four bedrooms, large gardens. Oh my God from being punched and beaten in the little council flat, my life had changed so much. But it was not all for the better, there was a price to pay.

As I settled into my little bubble Proctor would come back and create havoc, he would remind me where I came from, tell me my friends could see what I really was, his jealousy had become a disease, like his drinking, both of which he had no control over. He would become more and more possessive on his trips back home, and would drink in the afternoon, evening and late at night. He bought the girls presents when he came back, took them to the pub, becomes more unpleasant with the beer, but we would still have family days out, and most of it was manageable. Until he became very nasty and he would remind me I was from the gutter, 'Don't forget your roots, nigger lover. Maybe you should go back there?' He grew to hate my sister, referring to her as the 'Virgin Mary'. We were very close at that time: her youngest daughter is the same age as my eldest. We would spend weeks together when Proctor was away at sea.

I remember this night in November. It was cold and late, Mr Proctor had been drinking heavily, I hadn't. In fact I hardly ever drank in those days, especially when he was around. He had been very nasty, abusive, violent and aggressive, so I went to bed. I got in my daughters' bed because I felt safe there. I prayed he would fall asleep. I lay there terrified when I heard him come up stairs, I'm frightened and scared to breathe, he goes into our bedroom – all is quiet and I think he's gone to sleep. Next thing I know he is in the girls' bedroom he's bent down next to me, he stinks of cigarettes and alcohol, he grabs my hair pulling my head out of the bed. I don't make a sound, I don't want to wake the girls. He tells me to get out of the bed, I just did as he said. He punched me in my back as we left the room. I went to our bedroom, where he told me to get into bed.

'You are my wife, you do as I say.'

I am nearly sick with fear, next thing I know he is forcing himself on me. I am crying telling him to, 'Stop!' He puts his hand on my mouth. What is happening? Is my husband raping me? Can a husband rape his wife? I'm crying, he is cold like ice, my eldest daughter, four years, comes into the room crying, 'Mummy!' She is standing by the wall, I can't, I can't talk, his hand is firmly fixed over my mouth, he tells her to get out of the room. I don't remember her leaving, but it's finally over. I lay for a minute frozen to the bed in shock, he lit a cigarette, then puts his arm out to me. I can't remember the exact words that he said, something like, 'You're my wife and you sleep in my bed.' At this I stood up, feeling dizzy and nearly fell to the floor. I didn't say a word, just got in the shower then into my daughters' bed. He didn't come near me again.

The morning came, my daughter was uncomfortable and nervous, she knew something bad had happened. I knew I was pregnant – just that feeling. I made a vow on that day if I were pregnant, I would stay in the marriage until the child was at least one year old. I decided I was not going to struggle with nothing throughout my pregnancy, and whilst I was planning my escape. I also vowed never to sleep with him again.

Four weeks later it is confirmed. I am pregnant. I went to see my doctor I told him what had happened. He was upset. We have a great relationship – I was his first acupuncture patient during the birth of my second daughter. We touched on the abortion subject. He told me I would regret that for the rest of my life. He knew about my son and he was an amazing support.

I signed up for a home birth.

Christmas time is here. Mr Proctor has gone back to sea. He's sending messages, loving us all, and I fucking hate him. I didn't even send him a Christmas card, no present, and I ignored all his messages.

My pregnancy was a dream, no complications all the antenatal appointments were done at my doctor's surgery. I had the same midwife who delivered my middle daughter, we had become friends and she loved home births. The girls were happy, and they chose the baby names, if it was a boy he was going to be 'Joseph', a girl 'Victoria'.

22nd of July, I am up all night, even cleaned the table legs. We all know what this means nesting is complete. I had everything any mother could ever wish for her new-born child, and more. I made sure of that.

The morning arrived. I have even sterilised the bottles. I take the girls to school that morning and tell them they would be getting picked up by my friend. I met the midwife at the school. She could not believe I was out. We both went back to my house and yes I'm in labour. I am happy, relaxed, have been to all the relaxation classes, everything was ready in the house. I call my sister who is coming to stay with me as Proctor was in Japan thankfully, and could not get back in time for the birth, what a relief, I did not want him there.

As the day progressed, people were popping in and out of the house, the sun was shining through the windows, there was lots of laughter, midwife, friends, sister.

Prince Andrew and Sarah Ferguson got married that day and I gave birth to my daughter around 11:15pm. Whilst it was a long labour, I didn't notice: she was born at home and it was a beautiful experience. I cried, the midwife cried, my sister cried, my friend cried, this was a deeply moving special moment in my life. The midwife's name was Susan I gave my daughter that as her middle name her initials are VSP a 'Very Special Person.'

Proctor sent me a telegram, it said: 'To a lady and a friend thank you for my daughter.' I just threw it in the bin, and so the end plan begins.

Ten days after the birth I pick up Mr Proctor from the airport. The girls are so excited – 'Daddy we've got a new baby!' I could see shame on his face, he couldn't look at me, he knows I hate him right now and he is full of shame. We get into the car, did not speak: I missed the turn on the motorway I was so upset that he was home. He would see my daughter; he didn't deserve that. My brother was staying at our house and said he would babysit, I didn't want to go out, but didn't want to stay in with him either, so we went to the local pub, he drank and drank. I didn't drink. When we got home, he had more to drink, my brother and I were watching Marvin Gaye live in concert, I was looking after my daughter, Proctor went to bed. This was a very sad night. Eventually I went to bed, I won't let him touch me, and he got angry. He put a pillow over my face and he punched me, he accused me of having an affair with my own brother.

Time goes by. Proctor comes out of the Navy. We get a pub. He thinks spending more time with the family will get us back on track. No fucking way was that ever going to happen.

We have a pub in Saddleworth whilst still living in Marple. I have a two-month-old baby as well as six and four-year-old daughters. Every day I get the girls ready for school, cook chilli, Bolognese, and meat potato pie, rice and pasta. Prepare jacket potatoes, prepare salads, then drive to the pub from school, with the baby. I then serve lunches which was great and I loved it. I would pocket all the profits for me and the girls. I would leave the pub in time to pick the girls up from school. Get the childminder and then go back to the pub. Proctor was staying there, so that was great. I used to leave around 10:00pm every evening. I stayed at the pub with my brother on a Sunday night and Wednesday night, giving Proctor a break and time with the girls.

One Monday morning the phone rang the voice asked to speak to Mrs Proctor. 'That's me,' I say.

She tells me she is from the Social Services and there has been a report that my daughters have been left alone in the house at night? Well my head explodes!! What do you mean? They are with their dad? She tells me they had a call last night from an overly concerned neighbour, who had found my two older daughters at the front door in their nightwear crying and calling for their daddy. The lady stopped and asked them what was the matter? They told her their baby sister was in her cot crying, and they didn't know what to do, they couldn't find daddy. The lady was very concerned and tells the girls not to come out of the house. She waits with them, she tells them to get milk for the baby, that might help.

At 10:40pm dad arrives back, drunk he tells the woman to, 'Piss off.' And takes the girls into the house, he's angry with them for opening the door. He tells them he was in the shed all the time. I am not there so I don't know what happened in in the house after that.

I presume the girls went back to bed.

I close the pub tell my brother we are leaving right now. I took him home. When I got back to my house the girls had gone to school. Mr Proctor is there with my baby. He told me he had a babysitter, but she left because she had a row with her boyfriend. I spoke to my babysitter. She said she never babysat for him, just me. Then my friend told me he had been doing this for a long time. Almost all the time we had had the pub, some other mutual friends knew about it, but they never said a word to me. From that day they were no friends of mine. I told Proctor I was not going back to the pub and called the shipping company and said Proctor wants to go back to sea. As luck would have it they called him that afternoon with a ship.

Social Services came to see me, I told him what happened, they accepted what I said, and no further action was taken. Now the shipping company have a ship for Proctor he is going away which means I must make my move. It's time to leave.

Continuing The Walking Stick

And How I Feel Now
Carmen

LB can walk around the house without his walking stick. I think he feels comfortable and safe, plus we have adjusted the house to suit him. Outside is a different matter, the uneven pavements and roads – the surfaces are different. Whilst LB was in hospital, preparing to come home, I would visit and take food and sit with him, I used to do two visits a day. The ward that LB was on homed mainly stroke patients. The guy in front of LB was Chinese, he didn't speak English. He kept getting into trouble, because he kept eating sweets or anything he finds in his cabinet, but he wasn't supposed to as his stroke was different – to do with the throat and he couldn't swallow. He kept giving LB the thumbs up and trying to smile. The nursing staff were going mad. You realise that you're lucky in a way, he must have been so scared. I know because when LB did talk and open up about how he felt, it's about the things we fear and can't control. Simple things like going to the toilet, brushing our teeth, dressing ourselves. Also wondering if it's going to happen again. For me it was an anxious time, worrying how we would cope, would LB make a full recovery. He did. When we had a consultation with his consultant at the hospital, he said that LB was at his best, which at the time was about 75/85% and couldn't see why LB wouldn't have a good ten years. He has since been able to drive again. We have flown across the world.

The first time we went away after his second stroke was to Hertfordshire for a long weekend. We were staying with my bestie, who by the way had had three very bad strokes and is back to normal, 'whatever normal is?' Anyway, I organised the travel arrangements, the cab to the train station. Sorted the luggage. All went well until we reached Milton Keynes, which is where we change trains, we have to get to the other side of the train station. Oh yeah, its ok, we can get the lift, yes but when we get out of the lift there are stairs to tackle. I've got the big suitcase and the hand luggage and handbag; LB has his man bag. I'm being ten men. I can see how difficult it was for him going down the stairs, he was so tired. When we finally got onto the platform and found where we needed to be, he was exhausted. I went to check we were on the right platform and where our carriage would be. When I got back to him he just broke down, he was frightened and he couldn't help me. I realised that I had assumed he could do this because he seemed ok and I shouldn't have left him on his own. Once on the train he settled a little. We got picked up at the station. We did have a good weekend. LB was tired a lot of the time. We had to do that journey back home. Which we did. The next time we did that journey it was by car and LB drove. That's how much he has recovered. It wasn't all doom and gloom.

When he was having his physio and doing rehab, he was given leaflets on how to resume an active sex life. In illustrations; that was fun. There was laughter there was frustration there was success. The road to recovery wasn't easy, but he did it, and from what we have heard and seen he was one of the lucky ones. How do I feel now? Glad that's over and I hope we never have to go through that again. That sounds awful, writing about it tells me in the back of my mind now and again I must think about that time. It's an awful thing and it frightens me. But most of the time we live and forget about it, life is good, and right now I give thanks for the life I have. I feel grateful, I've got more than some and less than some, that's my life, I love life. I feel a strength and proudness in a heartfelt way.

I Have Missed My Heart

Tia

I have missed my heart. It didn't go anywhere. It just managed to become the master of disguise and presented itself as a warrior badge and shield for everyone who needed it. Or should I say, everyone I thought needed it. Under the instruction of a good friend, I have been sworn off Facebook for a while. The place that often takes chunks of my heart along with slices of my mind. My other friend tells me my passion is admirable, warrior like, but it should be channeled in a different way. So here I am, instructed by my friend and teacher, Linda Brogan, not to get, 'Too fucking clever'. I can't resist throwing in an age old cliche and writing the pen is mightier than the sword! And yes, it so is. Words, words in print, words in media text, words flooding from peoples' faces in Facebook fucking live videos.

I've been on Facebook for twelve years. I can count on my hand how many times I've aired dirty laundry or verbally crucified someone and given them a deserving proverbial throat chop. But I've never done a Facebook live. It could just be the Facebook friends I have on there, but they tend to be a little bit full of themselves, full of ego, even sprinkled with a bit of narcissism and some sadly just plain old, full of shit. Not all of them of course, but there's enough of them out there, replacing soap opera time at a rapid rate. Yeah, I could tap out and not tune in, so I suppose I'm a bit nosy but who can really resist watching a video of somebody you know and seeing if they've got anything useful to say or will make a complete tit of themselves?

When I took a week out from Facebook and vowed not to get into anything controversial, I was still reading everything but instead of answering back I opened a Word document and aired my thoughts there. Because I was doing this it made me more observant of how men and women were responding in particular to statuses around sexual assault. There were a few men that felt it their responsibility to post about celebrity idols that had now been smeared by sexual allegations. To me, their posts felt quite domineering, angry, dismissive of any alternative explanations, but demanding to be heard as if they were the injured party. It did cross my mind, did these men invite the discussion as merely a friendly debate or was it a possible reflection of themselves? Let's face it, we all sympathize, or even empathize and identify with someone that is like us in image or in attitude to the world.

I notice that my age was a significant factor in the responses I got when I had previously dared to occupy the male space. I had wanted to offer my thoughts – that extended the 'likes' and simple, 'Yes, Gee, I agree,' simplistic statements. The twenty something year old males tended not to respond to me. This could have been because they saw me in the same age group as their mothers or they were simply blanking me because I offered a difference of opinion. Commenting on men's posts closer to my age group was like being bashed over the head for daring to speak up and out. There wasn't any swearing, or, 'I don't agree dickhead.' Or anything like that. But there was a general feeling of having what I was saying dismissed. One person in particular did have the decency to go quiet on the topic for a few days but then he was back, like no fucks given.

Facebook is very much like a mirror. There's an emphasis to show the world your reflection beyond your physical you; your identity, your soul and shiny self is presented like a window for everyone to peer through. This is how I had been using it. Its interaction is based on how clean and shiny you'll keep the glass for everyone to peer in. Which room of your world will you allow people in? Which individuals will you allow in? It's interesting that Facebook now has rooms as I'm likening this virtual world to a whole house. I have not been in these Facebook rooms, so I don't actually know what they are about. I'm a bit of a snob like that – if something new comes out and everyone goes crazy about it, I usually run in the opposite direction and don't use it. Like if everyone changes their profile picture to pray for Notre Dame, I'm definitely not doing it when we live in a world where a whole block of flats can go up in flames and the Prime Minister at the time can't even make an appearance.

I'm definitely an over-thinker. When we were all expected to clap like seals at 8:00 o'clock on a Thursday, incidentally I did not, Facebook brought out the new hug heart emoji. It felt like those that weren't using it were the ones not playing the game. The ones that didn't care. I don't play games that I didn't volunteer to participate in. What harm is a Facebook emoji? No harm at all but a subtle way of encouraging you to want to be like everyone else. Fuck that, I couldn't think of anything worse. When Facebook analyses our habits and emoji use, I'm kind of doing exactly the same thing. Some people love to show the world what kind things they've done and document every one of them. I'm of the brigade that does good in silence. If you're not an attention seeking little numpty, you can do actual good stuff in real life and not have to take a selfie with it and post it to social media. I'm never going to be told what to do by a faceless entity and I don't need affirmation that I am kind. How mad is that?

I am kind. Just had a flash back of an old man that I had been helping in the community. COVID-19 mutual aid support. I'd become a volunteer seeing as I had been made redundant. I had had a call from the woman coordinating volunteers, to ask would I get this old man his electric as he was having trouble getting his key to work at the local shop. I agreed. I went around to his flat, knocked the door and he answered. I have no idea how old he was, other than he was older than me, grey looking skin, a bad hairdo, but as the barbers are non-operational, I'll let him off with that one, plus mine isn't looking too great either. He is wearing a vest and a set of shorts and looks very much like Rab C Nesbitt minus the entertaining humour. I see his eyes flitter all over me, but I pretend there is nothing out of the ordinary and I let it pass. He's an old man, I think. I don't know why I think that should give him a pass. He tells me I need to go to Stretford Precinct post office to get his electric. I hold my breath as much as I can, and I swear my eyes are beginning to smart with the stink that is coming from his flat. He stands there like a Salford gangster with hundreds of pounds worth of notes in his hand. He tells me he wants £50 of electric and that I should take a taxi. As I'm trying to walk at least 5K a day, I tell him the walk will do me good. He then says I should then take some money for going. I tell him it's very kind but there is no need as I am volunteering. Check what he says to me next, 'Are you stupid or something? Why wouldn't you take it? It's my money and I can do what I like with it.'

In my head I'm thinking, 'What the fuck.' This man is open to exploitation with this attitude, and after the stink of the flat, this is my second concern. I laugh out loud in disbelief at him calling me stupid. I tell him, I'm not allowed to take the money. I take the electric key. The weather is horrendous, so I try a closer shop. You may be reading this and thinking she can't be arsed with this old dude so why is she volunteering? Well, I actually also look after another old guy who is lovely. If I'm really honest, I get something from this 'kindness giving' because I don't have anyone elderly in my family. So, I think, in fact, I know, I attach myself to older people. Gosh I really did look in the mirror at myself this week, finding my heart.

Anyway, Electric man, we'll call him (but not for his vibrant personality) turns out his key for the electric meter is broken. The shopkeeper tells me he will need a new one so there is no need for me to go all the way to the Stretford Arndale. I get on the phone to Electric man and ask him who is his supplier. He doesn't know. I tell him I am going home to use the phone and the Internet to work out who his supplier is. I spend about two hours being passed from pillar to post. No one seemed to be able to find the address. Then it turns out he has given me the wrong name. I really don't see the point of giving me his first name that his friends call him and have a different one for his bills. I'm also tethered to the wall because my mobile needs charging and this long ass call is making me feel like it's the 1980s. As I'm stuck to my seat attached to the wall by the phone charger, I instruct my thirteen-year-old to make me a rum and orange. He does as he is asked but feels the need to ask, 'Do you really want a drink? It's only three o'clock.' I politely tell him these call operators are driving me to drink. I finally get hold of a half competent one who tells me she will send an engineer around to Mr. Electric's flat. I ring Mr. Electric man to tell him and he is so happy. He is so happy that he proceeds to tell me he is a little bit in love with me. I ignore it as sincere but laugh at the humor. A little later, Electric man rings me again and insists that I take some money for my time and for helping him. I refuse again and he tells me he likes me. I tell him I am just being myself. That last line though, just being myself. The self that ignores stuff, and inwardly seethes but outwardly appears positive and polite. He then asked me how many children I have and how old are they. When I tell him my eldest is twenty-three, he responds with, 'Bloody hell, how old are you?' When I tell him how old I am his words are, 'I feel bad now, you don't look forty-five.'

I don't know what that's supposed to mean. Yeah, I had bounced round there in sportswear and trainers and my hair was in a bun, so I probably don't look like the forty-five-year-olds I saw when I was growing up. I ignore his comment again and tell him to keep his phone line clear in case the engineer is trying to get through. He continues to be a full-on creepy guy by saying things like, 'I like you, no I really like you.' And other weird stuff like, 'You're MY volunteer now and I can pay you what I want.' I throw up a little in my mouth.

I got off the phone and my eleven-year-old says, 'Mum, you don't like that man.' I ask, 'Why, was I rude son?' He said, 'No but I can tell from your face, and your shoulders are like this,' and he pulls his shoulders up to his ears in a tense like pose. He's very intuitive and observant my No.3. On that note I instruct my No.2 to make me another rum and orange. I sit on the couch and stretch out my legs and make a joke that helping little old men is very stressful. The phone rings and breaks the peace. It's Electric man. This time he's pissed off.

The engineer has been, but he hasn't put in a new meter but just a new key. The plan has been for him to get a new smart meter. I said I would ring the company back. By this time the rum and orange has licked my brain. I get through to Gareth as an operator. When Gareth asks how can he help, I ask him if he is a real superhero and if his cape has been dry-cleaned because I am in real difficulty here, hanging on by my last nerve. Gareth laughs and tells me his cape has been cleaned and he is at my service. I explain that usually I am a nice person, and this is going to sound awful. I proceed to tell him all about creepy old Electric man and how my eyes smart up at the smell of his flat. Gareth promises me he will have an engineer return, sort out the meter and that should be that.

The next day there is still no sign of an engineer and Electric man is belling out my phone again. He tells me he has only £5 emergency credit and can I come and top it up. A feeling of dread fills me. I had told the head of volunteers all about him and about the bad smell. She then contacted adult social services who said he was only bordering and therefore did not require help as he was in that 'grey area.' She tells me she will come with me to get the electric. We go together and, on the way, she says something to me which isn't rocket science but makes me think. She said, 'When he kept saying all that creepy stuff did you not react because he was an old man?' I said probably. She then said, 'If he was our age and he had said those things I would tell him to fuck-off.' She mouthed the word fuck and pointed her head off to the side. I found it quite funny because she was a really tall, attractive woman in her forties, middle-class in a floral dress. I don't know why I think it's funny that she is swearing, but I'm smiling because she's definitely right.

We get to Electric man's flat and guess what? The fooker doesn't open the door. I feel like we are being watched from the window and because I have brought someone with me, he doesn't want to answer. 'Oh well, we tried,' says the head of volunteers.

Later on, Electric man tells me he was very unwell with the heat and could I come tomorrow instead? I agree. The next morning my phone is going. It's 11:10am. I've not slept in that long in ages, at least a couple of decades. Electric man asks me where I am because I am late!

I tell him I have had a late one, on the allotment, rock n roll, with a couple of mates and a bottle with the overly used sentence of the year, 'social distancing of course.'

Electric man's response is gold. I maybe should up his title from Electric to Mr. Class when he says, 'So basically you got pissed and now you're hungover?'

My eyes widen and my mouth is open in shock at his tone and I defensively say, 'I'm tired, that's all!'

'You got pissed! I will be the judge of that when you get here. I'm an expert at that stuff.' He says this like he is owning this statement and really proud of it. I really don't like his attitude. In fact, I don't like his words, or his stinky self and I feel trapped for being a fucking nice person. He asks me where I live. I tell him five minutes away.

'I didn't ask you that!' the cheeky Electric twat says. Not a chance am I telling this geriatric bugaboo where I live. Are you mad? Following this he adds, 'I've got a bone to pick with you when you get here.'

My fucking heart sinks as my mind races as to what it is. 'Fuck!' He wants to know why I told adult social services that he looked unwell. I swear I am shit at lying but I think quickly on my feet. Anyway, I hadn't told social services, just casually said it to the head of volunteers.

So, here's my blag of a reply after he asks me why I reported him as looking unwell to adult social services, 'I said no such thing to social services. How could I have said you looked unwell if I had never seen you before? I've got nothing to compare to another occasion of you looking well or unwell. I wouldn't know that.'

Thank fuck, he buys it. He returns to the question of where I live. I give him a nearby road name, and he asks where is that? I tell him around the corner. The cheeky twat then tells me, 'You have ten minutes then to get here!' I've not even had a wash, brushed my teeth, had a brew or anything yet. I tell him there's no rush as I am also with Utilita and that they never cut your supply off on a weekend or before 10:00am on a weekday.

Of course, Electric man has to argue and know different. He tells me that last Christmas he spent it alone without any supply. If he wasn't such a cocky twat this would pull at my heart strings. I know he's lying about no supply so I just say, 'Well it will still be on when I get there in twenty minutes!'

When I'm about to leave the house, the heavens open and good old Manchester rain comes in sideways. Fuck that, I think. He can wait. I text him to say I will be there as soon as the rain dies down. Laughable, he rings me to snap, 'Where are you?' and that, 'I don't even think you want to come and get my electric for me!' 'He's catching on quick but not giving up,' I want to say, but I can't be that blatant.

I borrow my neighbour's dog, a black Staffordshire terrier. She looks the part but not aggressive unless she senses danger. When I get up the stairs, Electric man is already waiting for me at the door of his flat. No hello, just a look of disgust and a,

'What's that?' I play that daft game of, 'What's, what?' Because I know he knows it's a fucking dog.

'It's my dog!' I say.

'I know that, but what happens now with that?'

'What happens now with what?' I say.

'You can't come in with that!'

'I can't come in anyway. Can't mix households.'

'Bollocks,' he says.

I ask him for the electric key. He instructs me to also buy him some alcohol and he flashes his wad of cash like I'm a stripper. I tell him, 'Can't do that. Sorry.' I probably could but I really don't want to. Alcohol has already left him in a literal stinking mess. He'd been drinking and pissing himself. No thanks. Not contributing to that.

'You're patronizing, you! You were pissed last night that's why you're hungover this morning!'

'Wow!' Is all I can say.

'Do you know what patronizing means?'

'You're giving me a perfect example of it now by asking me that.'

He laughs but he's not happy. He offers me money again. I reply no thanks again. And once more he calls me an idiot.

'Nice.' I say and I take the money for the electric and the dog and off we go. The heavens open up again, so I take shelter and I am definitely not weathering the storm for him. I'm learning in my own little way. Protecting my heart.

When I return, he says, 'You've brought a dog again.'

I sarcastically reply, 'No same dog, same walk. Just returning with your electric key.'

'But you can't come in with it!'

'I have no intention of coming in.'

'Why not?' he snaps.

'Because of social distancing. I told you.'

He tries to offer me money again. Tells me his son lived with him years ago and robbed thousands off him. Says he is, 'A nice person, you know?' He says it's up to him if he gives his money to me and no one else's business. He tells me, 'I don't like a lot of people.' (Who knew?) He says, 'They are all dickheads!' Well, I couldn't say all, but we both agreed on something in that statement. I can tell he just doesn't have the social skills to survive in the world and experience kindness.

I tell him, 'You do know there are people in the world who just want to help others and want nothing in return?'

As I am rummaging in my pocket for his electric key and receipt, I place my umbrella in between my knees. His words next, knock me rotten.

'That looks funny!'

'What looks funny?'

'That, there right between your legs.'

I feel his big horrible, goggley eyes looking at my crutch and so I remove the umbrella and slam it against the wall. He can see my demeanor has seriously shifted. I don't look at him. I'm too vexed.

'Here you go,' I hand him the key and piece of paper and I pick the umbrella up and tell the dog to come on.

On my way back I leave the head of volunteers a voice note, to say I can no longer work with this man and that he needs a male volunteer.

She leaves me a message saying she completely understands and that I should block him. I've got a shite phone. It blocks his calls but not his voicemail.

'I'm sorry if I offended you and I was wandering would you still be my friend?'

I keep him blocked. I've has a lifetime of trying to fix broken people in my life. I also think he didn't become a rude, creepy old man overnight. At one point he was probably a young, creepy man and I think about all the lifelong creeps. And I pick up my heart, dust it down and check it's still in good shape. I draw upon all those creepy experiences that happened, some as young as three and the conversations I have had recently with older women and I'm thankful and becoming content, that there is a growing generation of girls and young women that are beginning to look in the mirror, glossy eyed and confident with their, 'No means no attitude.' And they can say it once and not ten times.

Exit Strategy

Catherine

Proctor is away. First thing I do is find a job. I get a job as credit controller in an optical company in Stockport. This works around school times, it is short-term fix, whilst the girls are in school, baby is in kindergarten.

I get news that Mr Proctor is coming back early, he is poorly, suspected heart attack! I knew this was crap, he arrives home, turns out he has wind. He is not happy that I have a job. My birthday is coming up, out of guilt and trying to make things better, he buys me a brand-new Ford Orion car, which was nice and equipped with a top of the range sound system that pleased me. I could see the ultimate potential here.

Proctor sees a specialist on John Street in Manchester. They confirmed he had wind and he did not have a heart problem. He wants us to buy a bigger house. An old school has come up for sale and he tries to get me interested. I tell him I'm not interested. In fact I tell him I no longer want to be with him, I can't stand him. I have become brave now, he can't believe it, he's telling me what I am, where I came from. I look at him with such a lack of respect. I no longer care what he says and what he thinks about me.

It's my 30th birthday and I'm in bed. I don't want anything from him. My beautiful girls keep bringing me presents: chocolate, jewellery, music that they bought me – Whitney Houston's album. 'Please mommy let's dance.' We always danced together on Sunday, every Sunday, so I got up and I danced with them. *I Wanna Dance With Somebody* was playing and it was one of our songs at the time, we keep playing it over and over again. Their faces are happy, my heart is breaking, I knew this is about to end. I can still see their beautiful faces. All they wanted was for mummy to be happy.

Later that evening Proctor wants to take me out. I don't want to stay local so we go to Didsbury. He drives, says he won't drink, we go to all the usual places I know, that I'm familiar with, hoping I will meet people but there's no one out. It's a Wednesday night and I don't see anyone I know, so we go back to Marple. He wants to go to the local pub; I drop him off. Yes! I ended up driving. I go home, shower, relax. When he comes back, I tell him I want a divorce. Trust me that did not go down well. He told me if that's what I want I will never get a penny from him, he will not maintain our children or myself. I was okay with this, I didn't want anything and I went to bed.

Next morning there was the usual misery. Him smoking in the bathroom. Kids hate the smell. Breakfast, and school, and work for me. He hated that I had started working, so he stopped me using the car. He says he will drive me to work. For fuck sake that's all I need. He would drop me off. There would always be a row and I'd get the bus home. What a prick!

When he was upstairs one morning, I decided to get in the car and drive away. The car had an immobiliser which he didn't know about. I did this more than once. He would come to my place of work and try and take the car, but it wouldn't start. I would laugh. One day he was so angry he came into the reception area and literally punched me in the face, then walked out. My head was spinning. I walked back to the office sat down and said nothing.

I became very friendly with the sales director Brian. He was a lovely man. We used to go out for dinner, he would buy me a rose, we chatted and laughed together, he was a good friend, and had a wife and two children that he adored. He was a bit of a father figure for me. He played rugby at the weekends, went sailing with his kids. He was handsome and always smiling, the idea of an affair crossed our minds but thankfully we did not. So, we remained friends.

Of course Proctor would get angry when I went out at night. I did not discuss where I was going or who I was going out with. It was not only Brian, I would go out with girlfriends as well.

One night I arrived home and the taxi driver said, 'Looks like there is somebody burgling your house.' I looked up and there was Proctor wheeling my sound system out the front door. The babysitter didn't know what to do. I just pissed myself laughing told him to put it back and get the fuck out of the house.

He had stopped me using the car. One day I managed to get hold of a key. I went directly to Ford, and had nine keys cut and I buried them all in the garden. You can imagine his fury when I would say, 'I'm off now,' and jump into the car. He couldn't believe it. He would become more and more angry. The more angry he became the more I laughed at him. And I took the piss.

I used to climb out the window when he was asleep. Once he woke up in the early hours of a Sunday morning. He told me he kept hearing my voice, but he couldn't find me – thought he was going crazy. However I had sneaked out of the house when he was asleep, and gone to Sunset Radio where I was chatting with Hewan on his radio show 'The Brotherhood' which was a late night-early morning show. My voice was coming out of the speakers in the sitting room, as I had left the radio on. I kept that quiet, he never knew.

The house is up for sale. I'm driving him crazy. Kids don't really bother with him. He continues drinking, with his abusive behaviour, I don't give a fuck anymore.

Someone ran into the back of the car. Proctor had booked it into the garage. He got up one morning said he was taking the car to the garage, not sure why he told me? Evening time came, then the next morning, there was no sign of Proctor. I discover all his clothes were gone. Oh dear! I checked the bank. He had taken every single penny, left us with nothing. He'd put the car in the garage, written a letter to the owner, telling him to give the car to his friend. Well that wasn't going to happen. I went to the garage got my courtesy car, advised them I owned the car, they knew this and were happy not to release it to anyone but myself. They also changed the ignition barrel. I saw that twit who thought he was getting the car and told him the police would be coming for him if he tried to collect it from the garage. I said the car will be on my driveway, and it better not fucking move from there. He was scared of me and that was that.

When I got the car back, I sold it, cash in the bank for us.

Mr Proctor and I had a joint bank account: he forgot to tell his employers his new bank details which was a stroke of luck for me, as his wage got paid into the joint account. I remove the funds into my own account. Okay I can feed the kids now.

The house has been sold; I have to rent somewhere. Solicitors would not give me any of the money from the sale as it was paid into Mr Proctor's new bank account, in his name only.

Brian advised me to find a job in sales, where I can get a company car, commission and a salary. He wrote me an amazing reference.

I opened the Manchester Evening News, looking for a job that had no ceiling on what I earnt. I find one, 'LPG sales rep'. The salary was good, commission looks good and there is a company car. I apply and get an interview with the sales manager Neil. All goes well. Next round I meet Jon Paul, sales director of Elf UK. Just to be clear I had no idea what LPG was. I did a lot of research learned about bulk tanks, butane, propane, cylinder gas, rules and regulations, health and safety laws. I met Jon Paul and somehow got the job. It was amazing. I could sell my old car now. I was renting a house not far from where we used to live, and I booked a holiday to Portugal for me, and the girls. We went for two weeks before I started my new job.

Brian continued to mentor me, he was delighted I got the job, things were looking good. Mr Proctor has disappeared, no one cared. I had a new job, kids were happy, I needed childcare.

One day I'm in a dress shop where I knew the owner well. I told her I need a childminder, that sometimes I would be away from home. I can't believe my luck when she tells me her niece has been travelling but now she is back in the UK and looking for work. She is a qualified nanny. We meet she is lovely her name is Jill, she wants to work with me, loves the girls, they love her. She has her own room in my house and bathroom. I paid her forty pound a week and she worked part time at the AA. I also gave her a car, which I bought from the auction. This gave me the idea of buying small runabout cars from the auction putting them into the garage for work that needs doing, then selling them for a profit.

Jill and I would go to Brighouse Car Auctions, once a month, and would look around, find three or four cars to bid on, leave Jill there to do the bidding on any one of the cars that I chose. I would have a meeting in Halifax once it was over. I would go back to the auction, where Jill would drive the company car, and I drive the auction one, just in case it broke down. I would go straight to the garage with it for a quick overhaul and then into the Manchester Evening News for a quick sale. I gave Jill a good percentage of the profit and it turned out to be very lucrative for both of us. We lived like this for more than eighteen months, never hearing from Mr Proctor.

It was so peaceful. We were laughing, working, dancing. My social life was crazy. Jill was amazing.

Most of the friends I had whilst I was married were no longer allowed to associate with me, in case I led them astray! On the other hand, three of their husbands frequently hit on me. All our children still went to the same clubs, so we continued to see each other. A couple of close friends remained the same. We stayed in touch.

One day out of the blue Mr Proctor turns up...

Mr Proctor

Catherine

Over the next twenty years Mr Proctor continued to dip in and out of our lives always creating chaos and mayhem for example:

He turned up in Sandbach crying, telling me how sorry he was, and how he wanted to put things right with me and the girls. We all listened as we had done in the past. He assured us that this time it was different. My youngest daughter was around eight which made the eldest two, eleven and thirteen. I have been banned from driving. I had left my job as an IFA and was now chilling, cleaning, benefit paying the mortgage. We were getting by, better than most people in my situation.

I had just got my licence back but could not see any way of getting a car. Mr Proctor suggested to the girls that he take them including me to Disneyland. Well I was not going. I said it was up to the girls. He took them out that afternoon to the pub of course. When they came back they said he said instead of Disneyland he would buy me a car. What a result as the girls did not want to go away with him, and they understood the benefit of us all having a car again.

He told me to look for something and gave me a 5K budget. I stayed local. Went to the garage in the centre of Sandbach, where I found a three series black BMW, low mileage, one owner. Mr Proctor had to approve it. He came to the showroom particularly drunk, telling me if I want it, I can have it. Telling the salesperson/owner of the company whom I had known for years that he had been a bad dad and husband, he wanted to make amends. Proctor wanted to pay by cheque but I said no! He could and would cancel that. So he was literally frog marched to the bank, where he made a bank transfer to the garage over the counter. While I knew this would have huge ramifications, I'm back at the showroom getting the paperwork done! Logbook sent to the DVLA in my name. Receipt for purchase in my name. I can see Proctor sweating, thinking I'm going to regret this. We leave the garage, and I went for a drink with him. I felt obliged. All the time thinking is this really true, and waiting for the shit to hit the fan.

That evening he comes back to my house, which he said looks like a mortuary haha. Who cares what he thinks about our house? The girls, like me, are a little apprehensive, and wonder what he's going to do next. He got very drunk, started telling me he loved me and wanted us to get back together. I avoided answering and asked him to leave. I call a cab and book him into the B&B near the train station. I don't expect to see him for a while.

The following afternoon I go for my car. Proctor has already been there to tell them he had changed his mind. Unfortunately for him the car was mine, with no reference to him on the receipt or pending logbook.

Here we go! I pick the car up, bring it home take the girls for a spin. I'm nervous. Proctor turns up. He wants the car. I ask him to leave. He causes a scene. But finally goes. At 6 o'clock that evening I get a call from the BMW garage, asking me if I'd ordered a key, as my husband was in their parts department trying to get one. He said he had locked his baby daughter in the car and had no spare. He was also drunk. I confirmed this was not the case. Mr Proctor was asked to leave.

He had moved into the B&B so was lurking all the time. I went to work one morning, when I got back the house had been broken into. It was Proctor. He had ransacked the house, broken the glass in the French door at the back of the house. I called the police. They found him in the pub where he was asked to step outside. It was sad. He admitted to breaking into my house. He told the police I had stolen his car and he was looking for the spare key, which I had already left at a friend's house pre-empting this.

Police asked if I want to press charges? I say, 'No. I just want the window fixing.' He went to the bank, got the money for me. He was then put in a taxi to Crewe train station and told not to come back. A few weeks passed. We did not hear from him. Maybe he's gone back to sea.

One glorious sunny morning in August my youngest daughter and I were looking out of her bedroom window, admiring the beautiful trees that lined our road, the blue sky and sunshine. Even our garden looked good. It looked bigger. We looked at each other. Then we realised the car was gone.

Yep! Proctor's back. I decided to keep this low key in the house, not wanting to upset the girls. I called the police, told them my car had been stolen. Then call the insurance company. I was given a crime number, so the ball is rolling. I guessed it was Proctor, I told the police I thought it might be him. The policeman who came to see me suggested I just crack on with my insurance claim, as there is no evidence that Mr Proctor had taken the car. The insurance man came to see me. I explained what happened and they finally paid out.

Of course, I buy a cheaper car. It was bright red three series BMW which I call Victor after a local Manchester soul singer.

One morning there is a knock on my front door. It's Swinton police. They have come to arrest me. I'm speechless WTF!!!! And I'm taken to the police station, where I am shown to an interview room. They have found Mr Proctor in the car, which was reported stolen. He had told them I sold the car back to him, then said it had been stolen so I could claim the insurance. This is a criminal offence, and I could get locked up for it. All three girls are in school, so what happens to them? Mr Proctor had written a statement to that effect. I must defend myself. The documents were still in my name. I'm in shock that he would actually risk the mother of his children going to prison, or being held in custody pending enquiries. I explained to the police I owned the car, it was stolen, and that he must have taken it from my driveway.

They decided to believe me, as there was no record of any money exchanging hands or the car being transferred into his name. I am told I can go. Then I have to make my own way back home to fucking Sandbach. I'm fuming. I have got to get a train and I hardly had any money to pay. I said the police should take me back. They disagreed!

Another time he contacted me asking if I needed anything for the girls. It was uniform time, I said I need clothes for them, and he could do a food shop. We arranged to meet at M&S in Manchester. He didn't turn up. Surprise! He owned a pub at the time, so I marched down there, the pub was reasonably full, and there was Jack, who was our witness all those years ago at our wedding, behind the bar, with one barmaid. No Mr Proctor in sight. I asked Jack where he was and he said he didn't know, the barmaid told me he was asleep in the back. I went into the back and there was Proctor, he told me to, 'Piss off, I'm not giving you anything.' Usual shit. He went back to sleep.

As I was leaving the pub I opened the till and ask Jack and the barmaid to move. I took the money from the till, bent the wing mirrors on his car which was in the car park, drove back to M&S. Mission accomplished!

Proctor is full of false promises. Always giving with one hand and taking with another. Trust me, I learn how to hold on with both hands!

Once the girls were A level/university age they had their own strange relationship with him. He would help them with fees and occasionally give them money.

He owned the pub in Hazel Grove, where they would work for him and pay their own wages. Mr Proctor left the Navy and worked as an engineer for the NHS. He chose not to join the pension scheme as he did not want me to benefit on his death. Ironically when he became seriously ill with lung cancer there was no one around to look after him, so I did it. I did it out of respect for my daughters and I felt sorry for him. For twelve months he was in and out of hospital. He had a tumour removed from his lung, but he never fully recovered. I cleaned his apartment. Shopped for him. Visited him in the hospital.

June 2000. Mr Proctor's in hospital. I visit him. Tell him I'm going away for five days. I take him for a walk in the wheelchair. He tries to smoke a cigarette, but he can't.

He says, 'Thank you for taking me out of the ward.'

He says, 'Catherine you have been an amazing mum, a friend, a confidant, to those girls you are the strongest person I know. I was jealous of that. I always admired you. And please tell our youngest daughter, I am truly sorry, I am ashamed. I hope she can forgive me one day for the way I treated her.'

I went to Istanbul the next day. I had informed the hospital that I was going away, and there would be no one to look after Mr Proctor so don't let him go home. They did not listen to me. Mr Proctor went home that evening. When I got back from Istanbul on July 3rd (my mum's birthday) I had a knock on the door, it was a policeman. He told me Mr Proctor had been found dead in his apartment by a paramedic, who was delivering his medicine.

Proctor's funeral. As he was a member of the Merchant Navy I called them to inform them of his death. I asked if there was any help towards the funeral costs, and they say no but I'm entitled to his Merchant Navy Pension, as we never got divorced. Oh my Lord I was not expecting that! It's a small pension so I'm not rich.

Mr Proctor had about 10K in this bank, which paid for the funeral crematorium in Stockport and I split the rest with my daughters.

We arrived at the crematorium in a funeral car. Everyone is staring at us as we get out of the car. I can see this woman who I thought was Myra Hindley. She kept staring at me! Freaky!

We went into the chapel. There was about forty people, which surprised and please me at the same time. But that lady sat on the front row is telling Mr Proctor's brother and sisters where they should sit. It was strange. Once the ceremony was over, we went to his local pub, who had put on a white buffet. My daughters are talking to the Proctor family. They had never met them before, so it was interesting for them. Some of the cousins were there as well. My girls knew none of the Proctor family. It was good for them. My middle daughter was talking to Proctor's brother telling him how she had seen Mr Proctor at the chapel of rest and how he had looked. Then lookalike Myra Hindley chirped up, 'I went there. He was nothing like how you described him.'

My daughter was pretty taken aback as she had no idea who this lady was, she had become a little aggressive. One of the Proctor sisters asked her to stop. She wouldn't. It was then announced who she was – 'Proctor's ex-wife Beverley.' Wow!! Didn't see that coming. Their son didn't attend.

I was stood outside the pub saying bye to people when she came out with his sister and niece. I spoke to them said goodbye and thanked them for coming. I turned to Bev, and said I hadn't realised who she was and thanked her for coming.

'Thank you!' She said, 'You nigger loving slag.' Then she grabbed my hair, one of his sisters pulled her off me and took her home. I went back to the pub pretty shaken up. Told my family what happened. My youngest daughter has now taken her shoe off with a huge heel and is running after her. She wants to smash her head in with the heel of her shoe. lol. Families. Funerals. Weddings. You never know what's going to happen, or who's gonna crawl out of the woodwork.

Some weeks later we collect the urn take it to Weast Cemetery where we were going to spread the ashes. That's where his mum and dad are buried. We are stopped from going in, I can't remember the exact reason, however, we now have a dead body all be it ashes in the back of my car, so we decide to take them to Blackpool. He was born there during the war.

We get to the North Pier. It's freezing, and very windy. None of us want to pick the urn up. My youngest daughter takes it in the end. She is on the phone, telling her friend, 'I have to go I'm carrying my dad.'

Everyone laughs. We get to the end of the pier. Open the urn try to tip ashes over the side, they are blowing back at us. We are all running screaming, ash following us. We laugh at Mr Proctor's final gesture.

PPS

Proctor took the girls to Butlins. My youngest daughter came home with a rock dummy stuck in her hair, which had to be cut out and her hair cut short. My eldest daughter had lost a stone in weight, and came home with tonsillitis, she was sick for weeks. When we went to the doctor, he asked her to hold her arms up, she was so skinny her jeans fell down. The middle daughter had love bites all over her neck. she was thirteen.

He took them to Greece. The eldest girls were out every night drinking with a group of lads from Israel. They were fourteen and fifteen. The youngest had to sleep on a sofa in the living room and see him getting drunk every night.

I was in London visiting my brother in hospital. He had the girls at a pub that he was managing. They slept on a mattress on the floor. They ate pasties and drank sugary drinks, nothing else. There wasn't even a bathroom just a dirty sink and toilet. They took their white cat Mitzi. He changed colour. I washed him in the shower when we got home, I didn't know cats didn't like water and sadly he ran away.

One day Proctor turned up at the girls' school, they had told their friends he was dead. He was walking around the buses calling their names they hid under their coats.

He once went into school and told the headmaster he could not give me money for the school trip as I would spend it on men in Manchester.

He told the girls I had a black baby, and I went to clubs in Manchester where I would let men touch my legs under my skirt for a £1, fucking £1, are you kidding me!

For all his faults he taught me a lot, showed me a life I never thought I could live, gave me three daughters, he was hilarious.

The Birth Of A Fifty Year Old
Carmen

A sixteen-year-old mum, well sixteen years old when she got pregnant, seventeen years old giving birth to a beautiful premature baby girl, born feet first. Wow scary at the time, terrifying, alone in a labour room, poor mother (me) barely conscious. People, doctors and nurses, checking in and out, I don't know how long the labour went on for. A hard and long labour, as I write and really go back to that day in 1970, 4th August, I start to remember I've never thought of that day. The day my Lioness was born. Born 4lb 1oz – a fighter – she had to go into the special baby unit. The hospital was HOPE. Fitting name. This little bundle of loveliness, so small and tiny. Once I was discharged from hospital, which was after about ten days, I visited every day until I could bring her home. She was beautiful. Jet-black hair, the most enormous brown eyes, and the cherubic mouth. Like a miniature doll. She was in hospital for weeks. Once she got to 6lb she was allowed home. Home to me and nana, my mum. A lion and her cub. (Leo the lion) she is a Leo, strong, passionate, adventurous. Also, she can be down, depressed. A loner. Her life has had its ups and downs. I can't tell you her story, as I don't know it from her point of view, only from mine. I tell the story from my thoughts and feelings. And snippets of times in our lives. The struggle from her traumatic birth. Gaining strength and surviving.

I remember once when she was about two and a half years old, taking her brother out of the house. I was in the kitchen.

Next thing I know there's a knock on the door. There's a woman standing there holding their hands. She has taken him out in his vest and nappy for a walk. Luckily, the woman knew me and where we lived. Another time she put white boot polish on him, she was always up to something. She was also very protective of him. And even today she protects her siblings. Fast forward to ten years old, takes up running, becomes a vegetarian. She is brilliant at sports, also dances, helps take care of her brother and sisters. At sixteen boys come into play, she is very flirtatious. A boyfriend – her first serious one. She asks for the pill. Wow, shocked, but yes, we say. Her dad is shocked. At least she is being open and grown up coming to us. She goes through her punk stage. Then its Prince time, *Purple Rain*. She is evolving.

Eighteen years old. A young woman working at Manchester Airport. Also doing silver service waitressing for an agency. She started going out and partying with an older crowd, a major turning point. We found out she was seeing an older guy. I called her out on this, big argument, her storming off. Me finding out where she was at the boyfriend's house, going round there dragging her out. Her going back, a phone call from the police, she's taken an overdose of Paracetemols. Stomach pumped. Starts the life of counselling. Her depression; bipolar and SAD. Anti-depressants on and off through the years. Needs the sunshine, hates dark and darkness, for many years. Falls in love with a close friend of ours, she had a crush on him for a long time. They go out together, move in together, they are together for about ten years. He cheats on her and becomes a daddy (a one-night stand). She is devastated, goes to Turkey on holiday, loves it there, meets someone there, comes home and decides to go back to Turkey. Comes home and announces she is going to go back and live in Turkey. The person who she has met has his own agenda. He takes her passport, he is bully, she becomes pregnant, loses the baby. How awful, all alone in a foreign country. She is befriended by an English lady who has lived out there for a long time, and gives her refuge. All this time our daughter letting us think that she is doing OK. But then it's all too much, and she gets really ill and wants to come home, we send the airfare for her to come home.

Home even worse now, we tread on eggshells around her. She's up and down. Out one night and meets a really nice guy. He lives in Liverpool with his partner, they get chatting. He's solid, from a nice family, great job, shares a house with his partner, turns out they are not getting on. I think they exchange numbers; our girl is living in a little flat around the corner from us. Really trying to get her life together. Moving forward R and U meet again at a gig in town, and that's it. Within nine months they have moved in together, get engaged and married. They buy their first house together, lo and behold, she is studying to become a nurse and yeah she is pregnant. We hold our breath, finally she has a beautiful baby girl. They are great parents, both besotted with their baby girl. All this time she is still battling the demons. They are going through a rough time. It's a make-or-break time, more anti-depressants, counselling. She is now a cold-water swimmer, this has helped her so much. Made new swim friends, our mermaid. She has kept journals of her journey, written letters to herself. Had wars with herself. But all through this challenging time she has become a wife, mum, an excellent caring nurse, who will help anyone if she can. Finally found herself, finally likes and loves herself, this is my wish and hope for her. Earlier this year she wrote a post on her timeline on Facebook. It was about her abuse when she was a child, by a family member, who is dead now. She finally found the strength and courage to tell. As she said she hopes will help others. The shock was heart breaking, the anger was there, the hurt, the pain that I didn't know about it. Back to my girl, COVID-19, 2020. She said she feels like normal whatever normal is? At peace with herself. She still has the odd bad day, instead of every day being a dark day. These days it's probably work that upsets her. I just mentioned COVID-19. She has looked after patients with this and other poorly people. BLM met with racism from family and in the workplace. She is a strong activist for black people, for women's rights. For anyone that needs advice or help regardless of colour or race.

My beautiful strong, mermaid, bike rider, has hopefully found peace within herself and the dark hurtful thoughts have gone away. HAPPY 50TH BIRTHDAY XXXXX

Proud of this woman, Sad for what she went through. Did my life have an input/impact into how her life was? She is a warrior.

I've Got To Expect More

Tia

I'm not a religious person, but I know why pride is the biggest sin of my life. Growing up in Rusholme and Moss Side paints you in a coat of resilience, fuses you with a touch of hardness and a dusting of tenacity when mixing with the world beyond the Moss.

'Tenacity' – I learned that word when I was twenty-three. My sister was in a house share with students from her uni course and I'd been made redundant from the best job I'd ever had – a low paid pharmacy shop assistant job, but it was so much fun. I did so much that year, had a baby, split up with the dad, and moved into a council house on Alex Park estate. I'd go and visit my sister on Parkfield Street in Rusholme and I became good friends with one of the housemates, Keira.

Keira was a southerner, always expected more and got more. One of those girls who if she booked a basic hotel room, she'd find fault, complain, argue, justify, take it to the highest tier of management, end up with the penthouse suite. Whereas I could be offered a cardboard box and have to like it.

When her and my sister's tenancy ended, Keira moved in with me. I'll be honest, I thought her mum and dad must have been executing some sort of social experiment by letting her come to live there. This was 1998, the height of what the media termed 'Gunchester'. Not long before or after that time, I can't remember, we'd had some MP do a social experiment, living off a week's dole money and he miraculously survived. A load of shite really because it was one week. He didn't have to buy a new pair of shoes, or replace the detergents, toiletries or worse still have a fridge, cooker or washer break down and have to repair or replace it. So, you can see my expectations of a middle-class student come to live with me and 'surviving' were pretty low. Anyway, she survived three addresses with me: Sedgeborough Rd, Broom Avenue in Levenshulme and then Kippax Street, Rusholme.

In 1999, when fed up watching my sister and Keira slog over essays, read books and look clever, I decided to apply to do a degree as a mature student as I didn't have any A-levels to do it the usual way. Writing my personal statement was so hard. Who can working-class people turn to for help like that? Keira said, 'Write it and my dad will look over it and give you some pointers.'

In my head I thought, isn't that cheating? We do things for ourselves in the Moss, don't we? So, it's here the word 'tenacity' is given to me by her dad, Bruce. I had to look it up. I've learned not to be embarrassed to look stuff up now. We forever learn. Tenacity – a posh word that popped out of the statement and appeared on every job application I filled out after and probably will do in the future. Bruce was a clever man, a kind man; Keira was lucky to have him. He was the head of social services, somewhere down south. Another reason why I thought him having his daughter stay with me was some sort of social experiment. But he liked me and so I should 'expect' to understand that's why he was content to have her living with me. I say Keira was lucky to have him but really, if you unpick it, it is really an expectation, a given of life to have a solid, good parent.

The expectation of support isn't something that sits well with me and it's probably, simply fear. Take today for example, my allotment neighbour is picking some plums from my tree that I said he could have. I'm beavering away pulling two 8ft planks of wood and bashing them together to make bedding boxes. He shouts over, 'I like what you've done there. I'm once again impressed.' He's impressed again because last week I built what looked like a third world beach rum shack, all by myself. Quietly impressed with myself, I acknowledge the compliment because in the past I would have ignored it, which isn't a confident, self-loving thing to do. My sarcastic tongue can't help itself though and I say, 'Thanks, but there's something wrong with this picture though,' and laugh. He laughs and adds, 'I was just thinking the same but go on what's wrong with the picture?'

I reply, 'Role reversals. There you are gathering fruit and berries and here I am building boxes and bird defenders.' He then says, 'It's not actually role reversals. It just shows a willingness.' And then I interrupt him as I feel a lecture coming on. I still can't make my mind up if he is patronizing and prickly or if he is genuinely trying to help me grow. 'Yeah, yeah,' I say, 'It shows a willingness to do both roles.'

'No, not just a willingness but a capability.' And so, the lecture begins. He brings his plums and his man balls of knowledge over to show me how to saw. Did I mention I built a whole rum shack on my own last week? So now wo-man must listen to MAN. It's the height of summer and someone has actually let the Manchester sun know and it is out in full force and I'm sweating my mammaries off and I can feel my face is red, so where normally I would be offended, instead I stand back and watch him saw the thick piece of wood. He stops and asks me do I want a plum? (You know, the ones from my tree.) I laugh and tell him he is doing that man thing where he feels he has to tell a woman how to do something. He says, 'Not at all! I know you're more than capable. Sometimes people just want to do something for someone. That's all!' And that's probably all it is. I should expect a healthier way of looking at things. Not be a prickly cow. Although a bit of me thinks he secretly just likes to argue with me because he does it often enough.

Having recently connected with my heart and soul that I have missed; it's made me look at expectation. It was once a terrifying entity. If your expectations are safe or low, then disappointment is either reduced or avoided altogether. But where's the risk of the 'what ifs'? Where's the courageous, tenacious, Moss Side, Lancashire lass with no fucks given, gone?

I've never truly come out of my comfort zone. I've only ever done the dead certs. Some of the dead certs turned out to be dead hurtful, because you know, underneath you're a good person who deserves more. Always helping others and then being quietly disappointed when they don't see or do anything when you struggle. Barring a few lifetime friends from that statement. Hopefully you guys will feature in the forward or in another chapter, because I actually 'expect' to be published one day.

This time last year I fucked someone off, right out of the blue. Change in life isn't smooth. I dared to be vulnerable with a love interest and for a while it paid off. I never do long distance relationships and I never do accents but there I was a Lancashire lass wrapped up with a black Portuguese man, who lived in a beautiful little village in Cumbria. Twelve weeks of a constant smile, fabulous sex, the kind that when you have a flashback you get a stirring in the loins and it is very intense in that he's saying he loves me, after the third time of seeing me. Think I've only ever had my first love tell me he loves me first, so I am a little taken aback.

Tony is his name. Antonio, how Latin is that? He's kind, funny – although I think I'm funnier – tall, (I know, right) and can dance like no one is watching. The last time we went out was in Fallowfield and we took our forty-plus-year-old selves to a club playing all hours 80s and 90s soul and R&B classics and I admit the spirit of James Brown answered my feet and we were both just proper clearing the floor and made a bit of a circle amongst all the young 'uns. My expectation was always to have a good time or just a nice time when he was around. The last time I saw him, he stayed at mine. I had an event on at my allotment and as Tony was a chef, he had baked me two cakes. He was that kind of guy. It felt like he was totally just yours when you were in his company. At the tabletop sale I even introduced him to my sister on my dad's side, my best mate, and my people that I have mentally adopted as family, seeing as my mom and dad aren't around. That week after he had left, I felt like he had drifted, and those low expectations crept back in and yes, I did that insecure crazy lady shit. Previously I had rung him a few times but I noticed he never picked up, but he would ring me back an hour later. My head went into overdrive. I did the lowest of the low and finished with him via text. I can hear my own mother's voice in the tone I used. Told him he was using me, probably for a fucking green card. If you know you know. I never spoke to him again.

Lockdown, March 2020. And a few weeks after that Tony texts me, 'Hope you are all well.' No question or kiss and I don't know who it is because like a big baby I had deleted his number. No idea why he hadn't deleted mine because I would have been well pissed off with what I said to him. I click his WhatsApp profile picture and see that it is him. The Gemini in me says says, 'Aww that's nice.' And the other twin says, 'Dickhead.' And has a flashback of a Facebook meme that says '2020 lockdown has all the exes out, 'thinking of you' because they Goddamn bored!' Being somewhat of an addict of Facebook and of the law of memes and false information I simply reply, 'Yeah all good thanks. Hope you are too.' No question mark, no kiss. The lockdown weeks roll by and I wonder how the online dating world is going and has it turned completely to shit like all other small to medium size businesses. Nope it hasn't. In the past everyone would write in their profiles, 'Not looking for a pen-pal forever.' Now in these unprecedented fucking times, people are grateful just for a text back.

So, my profile reads, 'I'm on for date No.9 now.' it's probably Fifteen to frickin twenty, but trying to look like a classy bird by keeping it under ten.

There is absolute weapon behavior out there. I did actually have a date involving a butter knife. I think I could write a whole book on online dating, so I'll leave those episodes out.

Have a nosey at my profile to see how I come across. Opening conversation starter, 'Tia's Adventures in the murky POF pond. Get your tissues and inhaler ready for this ..... and I proceed to unleash the ridiculous and a couple of terrifying dates I have been on as well as a shopping list of what I DON'T want in a man.

Time to update my photos. I think it's a bit naughty if you don't put recent ones up. So, I pop a new one on and the dating site, Plenty of Fish (POF) keeps your most popular one at the front. The next thing I get message from Tony. 'Nice new pics.' Straight away in my head I get on the defensive and think, 'Fuck right off' I politely respond, 'I know, thanks'. Cheeky twat, aren't I?

Because he has sent a message I can see when he is online, and he can see when I am online. I am soon sidetracked by a different tall dark handsome 'new something'. 'New Something' and I go for a couple of dates, but he is too young not into anything serious. Couple of weeks later I mentioned to my friend that Tony had messaged me via WhatsApp and on the dating app. She asked me, 'Whatever happened to you guys? Whatever happened to Tony?' And she says it like I've buried him on the allotment. I told her my spider sense had kicked in and that something wasn't right. More like insecurity kicked in and I finished with him before he finished with me.

Another WhatsApp message from Tony. 'Hope all is OK with you x'. Yes that's a kiss. I'm in a good mood and so I throw in my Lancashire speak and reply, 'I am, love. Fed up with all this COVID shite, but I'm well, and so I'm grateful. How are you doing? X' And I'm mirroring like for like in kisses. He tells me he is OK, back at work. Oh, and how he keeps having heavy flashbacks of us. My cool reply, 'Well that's good you're back at work and I have no control over your flashbacks.' Insert laughing emoji. He inserts lots of laughing emojis back and says, 'True, I'm the one to blame. It's all good moments we had and a lot of them were hot so how could I ever forget you? Whatever it was, for me, it was all good.'

Aww, I have to be honest, and I reply, 'Remembered eternally? ...who can ask for more than that :) yes, no complaints here on the chemistry front. My issue was with myself.'

Thank God, he replied with, 'We all have issues.'

'Suppose t'is true if we're honest,' I reply, which is my defensive voice I use when I try and sound like a Manc Shakespearean thespian.

Here's his truth speak in response to my text break up, 'Yes if we speak out it will probably help to solve issues or feel better.' I have to just laugh and I reply, 'That was exactly my issue, not doing that.'

He kindly replies, 'I don't blame you and please don't blame yourself. There are many factors in this world that we unconsciously pass on. Once we recognize it in ourselves, it can only get better.'

I forgot how in tune he was with emotions. He hadn't had the best of upbringings and he truly wore his heart on his sleeve, and he did let his love flow. We exchanged more pleasantries and the next day he texts me again to say, 'It was nice to clear the clouds between us. At least that's how I feel. Keep it real and if you ever feel like dancing then you know where I am.'

I change my profile picture on WhatsApp the next day. I'll be honest, attention seeking. He comments it's nice and that I have lost weight. There is a lot of to-ing and fro-ing about fat swaps for muscle and that I've taken up jogging in lockdown and then Mr. Slim but muscley tells me he's gained a tummy. I say I don't believe him I'd have to see it. More laughing and joking and he offers to show me. Not by picture but says he would have to in person. A couple more exchanges and then he sends me this... 'Let's be straight.....suddenly we start chatting again and now we are feeling though we could spend some time together and

I think that would lead to much more than a catch up thing.... do you get what I mean? We have to think about it....I'm just trying to be careful before anyone gets hurt.' And he has used the Royal We so he's not putting it on anyone and knows then, I can't get defensive.

I reply, 'I get you respect clarity and are you avoiding that happening?' Go on girl I say in my head fearless and tenacious is back. Expecting more and asking has taken up residency in my mind and soul.

'You know I like to just flow and that would be creating conflict with myself.' There he is, being vulnerable and he said it out loud, well via WhatsApp, but he's open in real life too. I bravely reply, 'If we are both single then it will be whatever it organically becomes.'

'Exactly! I had a lot of thoughts about you and you have marked me.'

'Wow! 'Marked' you. Well, you were the only person I bothered to ever introduce to anyone, so you probably imprinted on my soul.'

'No pressure, but I think we have to meet again,' he says.

Signing off with, 'This time I will expect more.'

Did My Life Have An Input/ Impact On How Her Life Was

Carmen

Out of my children, our eldest daughter, is the one who looks like me the most; apart from our colouring, and hair texture, she is a mini lookalike. Same height, both wear glasses from a very young age. Probably about the age of seven. She wears contact lenses also. From an early age, she was Miss Independent, I suppose being the eldest child she saw things different from the younger kids. I'd say from about the age of ten/eleven she started to change – periods, boys. Getting ready to go to high school. I would be out at the weekend and my mum would babysit, have our eldest overnight sometimes. I found out, when she was older that my mum would be horrible to her, say horrid things to her. Tell her not to tell me. History repeating its self. That's what my mum did to me when I was about the same age. Already a pattern forming, and I didn't see it, I didn't see a lot of things. Do I think my life had an impact on hers? For sure. When she was in her twenties she knew, defo in her thirties. Going to the prison to see her dad, getting searched (me not her), her dad's affairs, me staying with him. The parties, going out at the weekends. My drinking, my smoking. All the time her own battles were starting and I never noticed. Seeing me battle and argue with my mum, but still have her in my life, our lives. All the time hiding her own feelings and emotions. Too scared to tell, she was so beautiful and still is.

At fourteen she decided to stop eating meat and become a vegetarian, which she still is. From her late twenties she has battled with food, weight going up and down. Stemming from a troubled childhood, I think. Now a strong-willed woman she has come from the depths of despair. Wanting to take her life, which she has told me she could do and do it properly. Although she has gone through so much pain, hurt and turmoil, she has finally found some kind of peace and loves herself, by doing a lot of soul and heart searching. Her love of exercise has had a lot to do with her recovery, counselling, her cold-water swimming, her swim buddies have become friends and family. Her love of travelling, seeing the world, buying and owning her home, driving and her motorbike. Passing all her nursing exams, she tells me how proud she is of me changing my life, going to college, passing so many exams and tests, getting on a plane with her to see her brother, our son, get married. I think my input/impact was to show her, how loved she was and is, that no matter what you go through in life, we can win, can be strong to fight the battle. Not to lose sight of our ourselves. He who has stood by her through some of her darkest times is her wonderful husband who came into the family not knowing us at all, a different culture, way of life, food. He was a shy young man, between them, they have given us a beautiful granddaughter. They have both been victims of colour, for her in the work place, for him within his family because of his wife. She has a life now, hopefully a long and happy one, where the good days are good and the bad days are very few.

WE put our glasses on each day hopefully there is a clearness that we see through these frames we wear, not for vanity but for clarity. They are not rose tinted.

Plum Balls

Tia

It appears the pandemic offered an opportunity for a plandemic for some. Many saw it as a welcomed opportunity to slow down and breathe. Others were pushed out of comfort zones and had to adapt and then there were those that were normally and often troubled on this earth and they found that the world was still spinning around and that their resilience had served them well. I think I went through a bit of the latter. I was OK. I was calm and losing my job came as a bit of a relief. Lockdown was made more than bearable because I was constantly on my allotment, my garden I'd never had. Being there more often, I saw one of my allotment neighbors more regularly than usual. For three years I've been entertained by the best soul music on his speaker box and he was an intelligent man so conversations about Doris and the Tory party, new world order and the occasional discussion on a conspiracy theory, were never dull. His jokes were bad though. They were that bad, they were almost funny and being the pedant, he is, he would argue that his humour was by design; it definitely is. There is only one Mr. Plum Balls. I don't think I know anyone like him.

I've got a few schemas in my head about men; the good ones, the bad ones and the bloody awful ones. But I don't know where he sits. He will always champion women's rights and I've been on two Black Lives Matter protests with him. So, we've been good friends for a long time. I say I don't know where he sits because of what happened a couple of months back.

I had been told by a couple of friends he had a soft spot for me, and I had purposely dismissed it because he had a girlfriend. 'Partner' he called her (he's terribly posh for the most part, not my usual taste in men). 'Girlfriend' I would correct him, when he did mention her which wasn't very often and then he would correct, 'She's my partner'.

'But you don't live with her,' I'd argue again. I had no idea he had this partner because for the last three years he had taken a picture of me every summer on my hammock when I dared to get my mixed-race moon legs out. I went absolutely ballistic at him: which I think he gets a real kick out of, me going off on one. Every time he'd say he would delete it from his phone. Every summer he would send it again to do my head in. Two years ago, he asked me to go to the cinema with him. I don't know about you but I'm old school and I still equate cinema dates as a date-date. Although I had said yes nothing ever came of it and we didn't go.

While toiling the soil, spitting feathers, sweating my mammarries off, Plum Balls and I are discussing how sex is now illegal. He tells me, 'The amount of couples who do not live together are going to find this difficult.'

'Pah,' I dismiss his remark and continue to tell him that, 'If I had a man I didn't live with, say he was abiding by this, he'd be getting dashed. No discussion.'

I had said this before he had told me, 'My partner is completely isolating.'

I said, 'What from, you?'

He said, 'Yes.'

And I slapped my face to hide my laugh for putting my foot in it. 'Oh dear, good luck!'

'You're cruel,' he says.

I then say, 'See, she's definitely your girlfriend then and not your partner.' Followed by the usual tit for tat arguing over what his relationship status was. I end it with, 'Call it what you want. It's all subjective anyway.'

I'm still doing what I'm doing which is I think what we loosely and carelessly call, seeing someone. Jordan, yep, 6ft and black, comes to the allotment every once in a while, has a few beers, moans about everything. I sit like a therapist listening to him 'til he feels better and then I don't see him again for ages. Got to admit, the thought of sex being illegal makes me feel like a class A escort doing extras, so one day me and Jordan get down to it and break the law at his. Just to think four weeks earlier there wasn't this law to break.

Plum Balls sees Jordan with me. Sends me a cryptic message, 'Whose your friend?' I reply by correcting his spelling of 'who's'. I do this because this is the sort of shite he does to me so it's nice to return the favour. Sometimes Jordan saw the messages from Plum Balls come through on my phone. Jordan also says, 'I think he has a thing for you.' And then like a typical male not really into you, Jordan increases his visits. That and let's face it, it's lockdown and he's bored.

Plum Balls would be in his shed or greenhouse but wouldn't have his music on if I had Jordan around; Batfink ears probably straining to hear the conversation. A couple of weeks later I get a message from Plum Balls and it's definitely more risqué than normal and wait for it, tells me his 'partner' has given him a free pass.

'A free pass for what?' I ask. He goes all around the houses to tell me his woman is literally two metre distancing from him, so basically, she's given him a pass probably to alleviate his ripened, about to explode plum balls.

I'm on the white rum. It's the day before my birthday and I've not got any plans (it's lockdown, after all) I think sod it, he likes me, I like him; this will get done, out of our system and that will be that. No, not quite. We do the do at his. No complaints from me. Definitely no complaints from him because he is asking for part two.

I have all these murderous feelings come up of what a using little bastard he is. Tell him I think he's a liar and I'm in turmoil with myself because I think, why haven't I had these feelings or standards before I did the do? And then what? Part two does take place. I justify it because one, I like him, and two, it could be on top of having to find somebody new. Jordan is beautiful looking, but he moans way too much and six months prior to that he had found out his ex was getting married. Yep, friending me off but also wanting friends with benefits. I lost any attachment to him after that, but I don't think he even realised because he was too busy moaning about how unfair life was. Plum Balls wasn't like that; pretty much always positive and found a resolution for everything. I've seen him annoyed only once but his swearing was hysterical because he just never ever reveals that side of himself. So, I am drawn to him and his bright white teeth and really dark skin and although he's missing the height, he makes up for it in his big, caring personality. And then what: part three, four and five take place in a week.

Part six is difficult, because that day, I had been arguing with a Z class rapper on social media. This guy had taken advantage of me aged fourteen — fifteen, so I revert mentally back to this time. And I'm viewing all males (except my kids) as using and abusing predators. Part six with Plum Balls ends in tears halfway through the do.

I'm broken from the inside about what happened three decades earlier. It's not pain that surfaces all the time, but it definitely was more pronounced and was more entangled because of the situation I was in. I started on Plum Balls again via text and phone calls. Told him about himself. Even brought race into it, saying he was putting his white partner on some pedestal of superiority by using me as an instrument. I think I blocked everything he said out, other than 'absolutely' and 'not at all' and 'I think highly of you'.

Part seven happens, and I tell him this is the very last time. He asks why and I tell him I want someone just for me. His voice is soft, always, never loud and the opposite of his basey little speaker box he has on the allotment. He says he understands that, 'And that we don't know what the future holds.' I tell him I'm not interested and that I would never trust him and, 'We have nothing if we don't have trust.'

I go on another couple of dates with someone not lacking in height, but attachment avoidant and momentarily I think, 'For fucks sake'. But then I look at how happy I've become over the last few months. I'm content. Plum Balls and I are still ok. He visits my plum tree, stuffs his face and asks me do I want one and now I just laugh in my head that he's one man I've had a chapter with and not hated by the end of it.

If you're wondering why I had seven parts to this rendezvous; it's because it was a six pack of condoms and we just made it to the second.

Stay safe people.

Time To Take Stock
Catherine

After leaving my job as an IFA, then living on benefits you may remember I became a cleaner to make ends meet, as well as working in a bread factory on the occasional Saturday/Sunday/Monday morning. twelve-hour overnight shifts paid double money.

I soon set up my team, so they did all the heavy work, and I did the organising. This was an awful job, such hard work, would you believe my partner was a doctor! I think he got off on knowing that I didn't have much money and claimed benefits. Making him believe he had control. He would throw the odd couple of £ now and then, reassuring his sick sense of self-importance. I suspect that is why I used to cheat on him all the time he was such a little prick with a huge ego.

One day I decided to get a full-time job, I applied for a local receptionist role in Chelford Cheshire. I saw myself sitting at a reception desk, answering the phone whilst painting my nails.

I was greeted by an American lady, she was mad as a hatter, she hugged trees, she once told me that she had been shot by gangsters in America. She drank cheap gin from Quick Save in Alderley Edge.

I was offered the job, and now find myself working in an awfully expensive dating agency.

I've been working here for a couple of years now. I love it. I started in the office signing up new members then matching them with like-minded (members) if we could find one. If not we matched them with anyone. From there I help set up the call centre where I managed a team of thirty staff along with my new partner. I have earned the trust of the owner CEO Mr Chris and worked closely with him on several projects. I became a strong member of the team and took over the events department. Generated huge amounts of revenue via the voice mail system and became Business Development Manager for the on-line and telecoms companies Chris had set up.

All this time the American lady was still telling stories, drinking cheap gin, and hugging trees. She was the general manager and had grown to dislike me, but that was fine. She once announced to the call centre that I had been allowed to buy a new kettle for the office because I was sleeping with the boss.

Through the grapevine I had heard the accounts department had been getting calls from the DHSS, they were asking about Catherine Donohue – of course no one knew who she was, after a year or so they asked for all the employees' full names, address and NI numbers, they finally tie up Catherine Proctor/ Donohue as one person.

I get a call from the accountant who also didn't like me because he was friends with the American lady, and I was friends with the CEO. It is all about company politics well I am sticking with the CEO. He told me what was happening with the DHSS and suggested I leave. I said nothing walked out of his office and went to see the CEO that evening and told him about my conversation with the accountant.

He was shocked, he called the accountant to his office asked for all the information and told him he was to have nothing more to do with this situation. I would not be leaving. DHSS got in touch with me. They stopped my payment. I was shitting myself I know this is seriously frowned upon, it was during the time the government were having a crackdown and sending people to prison especially women making an example of them.

DHSS arranged a meeting with me, I get to the building where I am shunted to a room with two, not so easy on the eye, or pleasant, women. They are asking me questions which I decided not to answer so they let me go.

Next time I arrive I have arranged for a solicitor to come with me. I find out on the day that she doesn't drive, she is somewhere in Manchester, I am at the meeting in Crewe, she has not prepared a case and now she has missed the train. What a twit, so the second interview has been cancelled. DHSS are not happy.

CEO and I are talking one evening. He invites the company lawyer to join us, and she suggests a lawyer in Manchester her name is Sarah. I go to meet her we go through the details, the simple truth is I did not tell the DHSS I was working full time, so I am up shit street without a paddle. Sarah is really upset. She tells me I will go to prison; I owe £37,000, and advises me to be prepared and get my shit in order.

I go home that evening and decide not to panic. I wait to speak with CEO the next day and we put our plan into place. The company will pay my mortgage, and all my household bills. My friend will look after my daughters, the eldest one is nineteen. She is at uni and will come home as much as she can. My middle daughter is eighteen and my youngest is fourteen legally they can stay in the house on their own, but they need some help and supervision.

I have decided to look for another school for my fourteen-year-old as it will be a heavy burden for her to bear once her schoolmates find out her mum is in prison. I meet with the headmaster of the school, I must let them know what is about to happen, he is both shocked and upset. He has tears and offers any help he can. We agree changing schools is the right thing to do.

I carry on working: the accountant is still wanting to know what is going on. Fuck him!

I have to tell my girls what I have done and what is about to happen. They are mortified, crying, upset, shocked the house is a very distressing place to be. I am full of guilt and remorse for what I have and am about to do to them. We discussed our plan and put it into action, all the bills and mortgage are transferred to the company for payment. My middle daughter decided she would defer going to university for a year, and school is sorted for my youngest.

All this in place I decided to book a holiday. (Who the fuck would do that?) We went to Greece. Before we go, I meet the solicitor, she tells me to get as many character references as I can from upstanding pillar of society type people.

I spoke to the headmaster, the operation manager of the dating agency, my ex doctor partner he finally came in handy, a couple of close friends holding senior positions and of course the infamous Mr Proctor. I get the references. Reading them made me cry.

Victoria and I go and see Proctor, as his reference was not good. Sarah has told me to write it, and get him to sign. He was sitting there, pontificating, and he is letting me know my true colours have come back to haunt me. Victoria is already upset and tells him to, 'Shut up. Don't talk to mum like that you didn't look after us.'

I managed to get him to sign what I have written. He is now saying he will stay at my house and take care of things. Which I ignore. The letter is on the table, we are in a pub. I know he can lift it up any minute. I'm trying to be nice. I want to cry with fear as his statement is very important to the case.

He tells us he's going to the loo, as soon as he moves I pick up the statement put it in my pocket, we leave before he gets back. Vics and I run to the car, once we are in the car I cry.

I take the statements to Sarah; she tells me Channel 4 are doing a programme on women in prison. They've called her, and said they are looking for someone a little different, she asked if I would be interested in taking part. I tell her I will let her know.

The following day. I speak to the CEO. He loves the idea, said it will follow on from what he is planning to do: if I go to prison he's going to the MEN where he has contacts, call Look North West and Granada Reports, he then asks me to call Sarah and set up a meeting. I go back to Sarah and ask her to set up a meeting with Channel 4. I meet a lady. Her name is Polly. She is lovely and a little taken aback at what I done. We are not here to be judged I remind her. I arrange a meeting with the girls. I explain this is a programme that explores the benefits of sending mums to prison for crimes that can be dealt with in other ways. It also shows the direct impact it has on their families.

My two youngest are okay with it, but my eldest doesn't want to take part. She says what if I don't go to prison will it still be shown? The answer is yes! After a couple more meetings and my eldest reaction I decided not to go ahead with it.

We go to Greece; it was the worst holiday we ever had.

The first night we got bit by mosquitoes. Hundreds of bites between us. My youngest daughter had seventy-two bites just on her face. She was so poorly after trying all the treatments that didn't work I had to get the doctor. We both had to have hydrocortisone injections twice a day for four days. He wanted to take my youngest to hospital, but I kept her with me. On day six she was feeling a little better. That day was also her birthday. I had booked a trip to the water park. She and her sister came down the slide on a double ring which popped. They smashed heads and went under the water, where they had to be rescued. We then had to wait three hours for the bus back to the hotel. It was so miserable, when we got off the bus, my youngest realised she has left her hat behind, which I bought her for her birthday. We are flying home the next day so that was the end of that.

Back home CEO and company lawyer have contacted my lawyers regarding paying the money back to the DHSS. They would not accept it. They offered to pay the money back to them on several occasions, but each time the DHSS refused to take it. My solicitor advises us to get a barrister, which I do. Again,

I am told I will go to prison. They are just trying to minimise my sentence.

It's the evening before my court case. I'm in Crown Court.

I have some friends around to my house. My sister comes. She stayed with me. We all drink wine, eat nibbles. I'm about as anxious as anyone could be that night. I do not sleep at all.

Morning is here, I wear a black suit and a purple shirt. My girls dress. My sister is ready. And my friends arrived. One of them has booked a table in a restaurant just in case I am free. We leave the house: three cars, six of my friends, my three daughters, my sister.

We arrive at the court, suddenly I lose it. I started shaking, crying, dropping everything. I can't do this! My girls hold my hand, my sister hugs me and we walk into the court. The wait goes on forever.

My solicitor, barrister, and company lawyer who still has the cheque for them. She gives it to the barrister, who again tries to stop the trial.

DHSS say, 'No'.

My solicitor cannot look at me. We both have tears in our eyes. Company lawyer promises me they will take care of everything. CEO is not in the UK he calls me. I can't even speak to him

Back to the girls, my name is called and we are brought to a holding area. Right now I can feel how I felt at that moment. I sit next to my sister, my head on her shoulder, my tears are falling from my eyes, the girls sit next to us, I cannot look at them. What did I do to them? Why did I do it? I want to be sick, my head is pounding, suddenly my name is called. The people who are with me are told to sit in the viewing box. I briefly look up at them.

Then turn away. After I confirm who I am I am told to sit down. Someone reads my charges. I plead guilty. Then I am told to stay where I am in the box.

I know there are stairs behind me, and they will be taking me to the cells. I hold my tears back, and I listen to the DHSS lawyer telling their version of events. It's not sinkng in. By now nothing is. My barrister stands up.

She says I know I have done what I have done. I have never been in trouble. I have brought up three children on my own and my company support me and I will continue with my employment. She tells the judge, that sending me to prison will serve no purpose and she has a cheque in her hand for £37,000 which the DHSS have refused to take.

Now the judge says, 'Prison! Who said prison? Take it from me she will not be going to prison today.' That's what I heard, but I heard the screams from my daughters, I heard them crying everyone gasped I almost passed out.

The judge turned to the DHSS and asked them if they wanted their money back. Why didn't they take it? They were wasting a lot of taxpayers' money.

Me! I don't care what's being said I look up and I see my daughters, and friends, I want to cry right now, when I think of their faces that day. The judge asks for, 'Quiet.' He tells me what I have done is very wrong, but he can see how sorry I am. And thanks the company for supporting me and paying back the money. He said, 'This was brought to the courts I must give you punishment. Therefore, I give you one hundred and forty hours community service. I'm obliged to give you a twelve months suspended prison sentence, but I don't expect to see you back and I don't have any concerns.'

He tells the DHSS to take their money, and take a long look at what they achieved today.

Oh my God, I thank the judge, I meet Sarah who is now crying. We go to the room with the barrister and the company lawyer and fill in the paperwork. Finally, we are done. I meet my daughters, sister, and friends there are tears of joy, regret, sorrow, we go to the restaurant for celebration.

I think I drink for another twenty-four hours, then finally collapse. CEO calls me, tells me to get my arse back to work.

I love him. When I finally get back to the office, I go and see him in his massive room, with its oversized sofas. He stands up, we look at each other, tears in our eyes, and he hugs me, and he hugs me forever and now I feel safe.

I Do More For Them To Make Up For What I Did

Carmen

Who are they? My children, grandchildren. I think with the kids it was when they had left home and they would just say in conversation that they wanted something or money. I would do it for them, or I'd lend the money. Sometimes it was my time; I'd move things around to fit in with them. Why? Because I didn't want to say no. I didn't want them to ask anyone else. I'm their mum, nana. As they have grown older and branched out on their own, they would say mum you don't need to do that. I've had to learn they need to do things for themselves. So now I help with the grandchildren and great granddaughter. If they want to go out or have a break, picking up from school or nursery. I didn't really have that help or support. Today I was shopping and bought them some holiday bits, some canvases for their bedroom walls. I do this because I didn't have anyone who did this for me. It's making good and loving memories. I have to say these days I do say no. In fairness the kids don't ask us for money these days, its more childminding which I'm happy to do, or advice. I would do anything for them. Yes, I still try to fit in with them, if I can. If I can't, I don't. I like to make an effort on birthdays and Christmas for all of them. You know, though, I've seen through life sometimes that the worse you are as a mother; they love you just the same.

Big Bad Wolf: The Only Love That Bites

Tia

Do we need context to explain an exploitative event? Does it add or detract from the facts of the matter? Does it matter? I look at my upbringing and it's a myriad of contradictions. My maternal grandparents were married and so too were my paternal grandparents. My mum and dad were married but not to one another. I am the eldest child of my mother and the youngest child of my father's. My grandparents had all their children together and my father had children with three different women and my mother had children to four different men. I didn't speak about it often, but I joked, dismissed and made light of this fact. For all the siblings I have, which is ten in total from both sides, they're all technically half siblings. But my mum's kids and I were taught never to act like we weren't fully related.

Religion, I've never had one. My mother was a Catholic and said she had tried to have me baptized as a baby, but the priest refused because she was an unmarried mother. I heard her say to a friend she told him to fuckoff as he had baptized her friend's baby who was white. It could have been true, who knows with my mum. She exaggerated a lot of stuff. So, although she's a God fearing Catholic, she was prudish with some things and careless with others. Daft things like, she would turn the telly over if there was a kissing scene, (you know, two people showing affection to one another) but she'd let you watch Spartacus being speared to death in his side and crucified and that was OK.

My mother had been brought up in complete squalor and so she brought us up in complete OCD. The house was immaculate even if we didn't have very much. I sometimes wish I'd been hit with the tidy up and clean gene. My mum did say her dad was very clean. Yet the contradiction here is that he was accused of grooming his own children. It was thrown out of court and dismissed but it was still a massive thing to be bandied about and mishandled by the family.

I understand cleaning up too well, and to be overly organized, it's a sign of losing control in other areas of your life. So, I am quite content with my organized chaos. As early as age five, my mum would be sat with her friend and would be spelling out s-e-x. The most easy, phonetical sound for any five-year-old to blend together and work out and then be scolded for listening into big peoples' conversations.

As I became a teenager, I still can't work out whether it was a matter of luck or intelligence that I wasn't labeled little slut or slag. Slag always sounded dirtier, and looser than slut. Ha, the power of a sound. Being sexually active from young wasn't because I had an insatiable sexual appetite to feed, I think, well I know now as a parent, it came from not having a father present in my world. I daydream sometimes when I see a dad and a daughter together. That bond, they are almost equal standing next to one another; the Paternal Protector versus the Mini Princess that rules his world. It's a world I don't know and one I think I grieved for in the form of anger and promiscuity. Growing up, the men I chose were always old enough to be my father. Except for one. I'm calling him Mr. Y because he thinks he's so Class A and as I don't think that at all I've chosen Y To stand for the question, 'Why?'

He was six years older than me, had his own place and was in the music industry. Had his own little entourage made up of other artists, friends, wannabes and groupies. Was I a groupie?

Maybe. I wagged school with my mates in our school uniforms, tucked up with him on a sofa not even thinking any of it was wrong. This is the context. Grooming is not black eyes, thick lips and ripped knickers. It's slow. It's steady. It's subtle. It's not recognized in the moment as anything other than enjoying the moment. That's where all predators get to hold their victims to some sort of account. 'You enjoyed it.' So therefore no case to answer. Also, the time lapses. Did we have conversations about no one being home other than the two of us or did it just happen? I don't remember. I wish I did remember more but on the other hand maybe I don't. I do remember washing his back in the bath and his mum came over. She went mad about him having young girls in the house so often. Every now and again he'd have a clear out and say no one was dossing over anymore at his place.

Mr. Y absolutely loved himself and yes, he had the charisma to make you believe it. Only young eyes, I see now, would believe it. Now he smacks of intolerable bullshit and it's no surprise his now girlfriend is half his age. Him in his fifties and her in her mid-twenties. He always had the most stunning model-like girlfriend back in the day, same age as him but a good foot taller than him. He wasn't a handsome man but his confidence made up for that, which came across in his musical expression. He'd had a big row one night with his girlfriend and he asked me to walk to the cashpoint with him. We cut through Whitworth Park. It happened up against the tree. No protection. No love. Just sex. I didn't orgasm. He did. We walked back to the house. The girlfriend was there. They're back on.

That was my first-hand experience of seeing that a man could be out shagging up somewhere one minute and return home cool as cucumber to a partner the next. I could see the flicker on his brow and the inhaling of his chest. The poker face. Knowing this look has served me well in reading people. I used to think I was intuitive. Gob shite. It's actually deciphering responses to traumatic or difficult situations.

The next time he has sex with me, I'm not lubricated enough. I'm not experienced enough to know that and so I have vagina swelling that doesn't go down for days. It was so bad I momentarily thought I was becoming a man and was growing testicles. Science, biology class, was useful that week when we were taught fourteen days after day one of a period, a woman ovulates. I'm doing the maths and I'm quietly shitting myself until my period comes two weeks later.

Other than my closest friend, no one knows I'm sexually active. I survive not being called a slut or a slag but then I think could those words have risen alarm bells if a teacher had overheard? Then I think, no, a different time entirely. We often had boys older than us, pin us against walls, cop a feel of our breasts, jump on our backs and hump us through clothes with their tiny, hard penises poking through. I never ever told my mum, boys in our school did this stuff. I'm unsure why, even now. I think it was because it was happening to almost everyone and so therefore you didn't make noise about it.

Mr. Y has all us fourteen, fifteen-year-olds year olds in his music video. I wonder how many others had the same or similar experience of one-to-one with him? For the last few years, we have had the hashtag 'Me Too' campaign. It's predominantly been white female celebrities speaking out about sexual exploitation in the industry. But for black women, there appears to be this culture and view of them being sexual creatures, therefore how can it be abuse? I've heard grown ass men make the most ridiculous of defenses for perpetrators of these sorts of crimes. The most fitting remark on a Facebook live was, 'Why do all these women want to come out saying shit thirty years later when man's got a woman and a family?' That three decades later is me. I'll tell you why. Women like me have had to work hard at building themselves up from the inside, loving themselves as they should, shielding themselves from suspected predators, treading cautiously in relationships and creating their own paternal shield where a father should have showered her in enough love that his little girl should never have stepped out into the woods alone when the Big Bad Wolf was lurking.

We dare to open our mouths now, because we aren't little girls anymore but some of our past encounters torment us from time to time. Like when a celebrity is under suspicion of exploitation or a man is acquitted for rape because his victim wasn't holier than thou. And the biggest reason of all for speaking up and out is because for years we believed the lie of it not being abuse. It happened to lots of people so it's nothing new; it's nothing special. You even stay friends with the predatory creature because to not be would indicate your disdain for them and you would have to acknowledge the exploitation.

For thirty years I stayed quiet, for all my life I've quietly, inwardly, seethed. Mr. Y makes a Facebook statement. Tells all us Black Lives Matter supporters we are knobs for protesting, 'You need to go protest all the Asian paedophiles in Rochdale.'

Hearing that, my blood and piss, are truly boiled. I reply, *'Wow, how can you even say the injustice what happened in the US has nothing to do with the UK? OK, the US police have guns, but it was a fucking knee that finished that man off. Look up the deaths of BME in custody in the UK. Listen to the racism online from kids playing games. My kid is called a nigger often. I deal with his hurt on a regular. As for wearing masks, go look up the death stats of COVID rates in predominantly black countries. COVID is not killing them four times the rate of their minorities. People break their neck to avoid black men on the street as if they're not familiar with them and now everyone's avoiding checkouts with BME people or jumping out of the way of us when we shop.*

I protested last week, and I'll protest this week. I'm not fearing a single virus when the world is full of them. You don't quarantine the healthy, you quarantine vulnerable and sick. Calling me a knob doesn't hurt when King Dickhead is bitching from behind the keyboard.'

Mr. Y tries once more to justify protesting against Asian men groomers in Rochdale. I reply, *'I was groomed by both white and black men. Who protested for me?'*

No reply. Silence. I know he knows I've got much, much more to say but the Wolf stays quiet, waiting and waiting. My inbox pings with a message. My heart is in my mouth. Mr. Y? No. Another woman who has pieced my words together and read between the lines. It's happened to her too. Cigarettes and alcohol are the goodies offered for her to wag school at his place. Who knew that there were so many Red Riding Hoods peeping from behind trees, just waiting for one girl, one woman to lead the way and say, no this isn't right, and it was never right.

Back to the context, I was lacking in having the right role models, appropriate adult, woodcutter, that I could confide in. I lacked the father, or father figure to steer me away or escort me through the forest of life.

All women matter.

All fathers matter.

And the existence of Wolves, matters.

Chris CEO

Catherine

Sitting in the office chatting to colleagues, a chap walks in, he grunts, goes upstairs this happens most days. I asked the American lady who he is.

'Oh! That's Chris he is the CEO you're not allowed to talk to him. He only talks to higher management.'

I smile and say, 'We are a small company.'

A few days later he comes in. I am behind the screen of our makeshift kitchen at the time. I'm making tea/coffee. I pop my head around the corner and say, 'Good morning,' to him, and ask if he would like a cup of tea or coffee.

He stopped in his tracks. 'Who me?' He replies.

I say, 'Yes.'

'Oh well in that case, I will have a cup of tea. White, milky, and no sugar.'

I smile to myself, make the tea and bring it upstairs to his office.

He is sitting there on a large chair. He's a big guy approximately six foot four and waist to match. He has a pleasant face, a cheeky smile, he thanks me for the tea. I am intrigued and want to know more about him. I continue to make the tea in the mornings, and we start to chat a little more each day.

He's almost shy, but I know there's much more to him than meets the eye. We talk about the business: how it can grow, how we get new members, especially men, and we make plans. Offering memberships to male members for £99 when it was really £1000 pounds to join.

I recruit interviewees all over the country. Everyone who joins is met by one of our interviewers at their home. They write a profile about them and validate their identity.

We start an events team, for the members, and our first event is a ramble rally in Cheshire, through the woods. We gave them packet soup and bread and charge £10. It was a great success and now we roll them out all over the country, with the interviewers and me or other colleagues hosting them. We also organise dinners nationwide, and trips abroad.

Then came the summer ball. This is hilarious – £250 a ticket. Members of staff in the kitchen of a marquee on Chris' land. A five-course dinner, a harpist, table-top magician and a DJ.

The kids from my daughters' schools are the waitresses and waiters. All the local B&B/small hotels are booked up for the members. Members are drinking, dining and dancing. We are asked on more than one occasion if we do outside catering. The chef is a drunk. I know him from Sandbach, and the man who worked in our post room. We'd made pavlovas, they were all over the kitchen floor in the marquee. The evening is a massive success.

Two of the members went into the portaloo for rompy pompy. They get a bit vigorous the loo tips over, there's shit and piss over them. 'A bit awkward!' The events became a great success and Chris was hands-on, he loved being involved.

We get to know each other very well. Chris loved to shop so we would go together to buy food for the events, the five-course summer ball dinner, and hog roast on bonfire night, events in the office building. We occasionally went for dinner after a late night or shopping spree. We would bring pizza for the girls, along with chocolates and sweets: they liked him.

Chris was a great friend to me when I had a problem with my mortgage I told him that everyone in the department was being paid more money than me and I was the only one bringing in contracts. He instantly gave me a pay rise, a company car and a windfall for my bank.

He was always kind and always made sure I was looked after. He saw me as a confidant and told me many things he never disclosed to anyone, they stay with me to this day. He liked nice food, and clothes. He was immaculately presented, always travelled first class, had a cheeky grin and a very funny side. He was kind of a womaniser but, also a little bit scared of women. An extremely successful entrepreneur, when I met him he had a dating agency which was aimed at professional people. There were several famous names on the books.

He also bought a telecoms company from two guys in Manchester. They moved up to Cheshire and the company enabled Chris to grow his enterprise by employing only the very best in the technical and telecoms industry. They were the first company to introduce online gambling with the Sun and the News International. I changed all the phone lines to premium rate numbers for the dating agency making large sums of money for the company, which grew from strength to strength. The telecoms company finally sold to a large corporate, for so much that Chris entered the Times Rich List. I think he came in the top twenty. Chris was a kind man. He was often misunderstood, and lonely. He felt alone a lot of the time.

People ask why he gave me that £37,000. He gave it to me because he trusted me. He did not want to see me come to any harm, I was a good friend, a listener and he often confided in me. We had worked together on many projects. I made him feel human and part of the team. We sometimes flirted with each other but that was all. Maybe in a different time things would have been different? We will never know.

Chris died in a helicopter crash. He was the pilot with one passenger – his PA. Chris was in America at the time, I heard the news on the radio whilst driving to Stratford Upon Avon, with my then partner and daughters. We were taking my youngest to the theatre to see Romeo and Juliet, it was her 18th birthday. I got an instant migraine.

I was not allowed to attend Chris's funeral, his very ex-partner made sure of that. I know Chris would not have agreed with what happened as many of our colleagues did not. I respected her wish and said goodbye in my own way. Chris and I loved and cared for each other and we were great friends, to this day I thank Chris for what he did for me. RIP.

The House On Clarendon Rd

House Number One
House Number Two
Carmen

A house of ill repute. HA HA. A nice clean respectable road. Nice kept gardens big old houses. This house from the outside looked like all the other houses, but it had a secret. By day it was quiet. Oh by the night it wasn't. It was let into flats. J had the ground floor flat. From the outside it was smart: a winding path up up three or four steps to a porch with ornate tiles, a front door two panes of glass, leading into a large hallway. J had the ground floor flat with three rooms. First door on the left was her bedroom, next to that was another bedroom, then the kitchen come sitting room. J used to let the girls use her front room to earn money. Working girls, hustlers, street girls. It was around 1972/3. I knew some of the girls, from going out and about in Moss Side. J was a little beauty, waist length jet-black hair, very petite, she was seeing one of the big sounds men from back in the day. About three or four girls used to use J's house, I can't remember how I came to be a runner/cleaner for her. I think it was through one of the girls called Mary (not her real name). A red head, curvy, no beauty, but a heart of gold, really kind hearted, always looked out for me. About eight o'clock I'd go round and by then a couple of the girls would be there with J. J would go out early. I would make sure the rooms were clean. Get the girls brews ready, nip out and get anything they wanted from the local shop. There was always someone in the flat. I remember it must have been winter, as I remember banking a fire in the kitchen. The girls would sit around the table chatting. They used to pay every time they had a client. Once they had used the room I would go in clean and tidy up. I would check on the girls make sure they had everything they needed. They were very clean and always washed after seeing someone. They used to work Withington Rd, Yarbrough St, Alex Rd, Gt Western St, Broadfield Rd. Sometimes whoever was using the room would ask one of the other girls to watch or join in. On a busy night the girls could make £100 and sometimes nothing if it wasn't busy. When the girls finished working, they would have a drink together in the kitchen, then get ready to go to the Blues. Some girls had pimps and would work till two in the morning. If they worked weekends, they would try finish early so they could go out. They would go to the Edinburgh. Especially on a Saturday night, and then go to the Blues. J was very popular as she was a dom girl, she had lots of outfits, to dress up in, whips and crops. My first time as a working girl was with J and Mary, they showed me what to do, I watched them, I don't remember him, he was a big fat guy, what I do remember is the red light, silk bedding, being nervous. I wasn't the cleaner any more. I was a working girl. It wasn't long after this that I was taken away in a van. Mary noted the number plate rang the police. I was dropped back off in Moss Side, terrified, battered and bruised. That was the end of my street days. I often wondered what happened to J and Mary. I heard that Mary went to London. The streets were mean at times. You had the police to watch out for. Every time you got in a car, you didn't know what or who the guys were, and you had the local vigilantes. The one from Whalley Range was called Mrs Tippin and she had her husband running around with her. She would run you, take punters' car registration numbers. You had to hope you never got lifted by the police, or taken to court.

House number two. Funny enough it's right next door to house number one. My friend AJ lived on the top floor with her two kids. Heart of gold, hard as nails. So back doing a bit of work, it was winter time. We used to go in the cars, I'm out on Withington Rd, get in a car, go to Hough End Fields. Do the business and this bastard doesn't want to pay me. Punches me takes my money and throw's me out of the car. I walk/run home, bathe, get dressed and go up the Edinburgh club, meet the girls. A couple of months later, its near Christmas and AJ and I are broke, so we decide to work, but we have a plan. She will get a punter, bring him back to the flat, I will creep, which means while they are doing the business, I will creep in the room on my hands and knees on my belly. Lift the guy's wallet. After she has the money hopefully. He will put his trousers on the floor, which he does and I lift his wallet. I can remember how nervous and frightened I was. We did this a couple of times. The last time I got a bad feeling, I waited behind the door until she got out. When he had gone, we were going back out only we spotted him looking for the house he had realised what we had done. We jumped from the garden and ran. When we opened the wallet, it was like Christmas had come early. We bought our kids' toys and did a big shop and shared it between us. We had a great Christmas, but that was my last creep. You can image legs in the air, arse bumping up and down, you have to judge your timing, hold your breath, while she keeps him entertained. Heart rate is through the roof. You can't get caught, I wasn't a thief, if you know what I mean.

One Hundred And Forty Hours
Community Service

Catherine

After the court case I am told to report to the probation office in Crewe.

When I get there, I am mistaken for a lawyer. I speak to the probation officer, who explains my community service order. The dos and don'ts. And tells me what happens if I miss a week. Happy with this I am sent home.

I come back the following week, where I am given hard shoes a high vis jacket and a hard hat. They're all grubby, the other people there still think I'm a lawyer or probation officer, so I have to win them around quickly. I have a fag with them and chat shit. Eventually gain some trust.

We are put on a minibus and taken to a park where we have to weed, pick up litter, and do shit jobs. I get talking to the person who is in charge, I tell him the work is hard and the boots are hurting my feet. When we get back to the office for lunch, he calls me in he suggests I do some other kind of work and gives me a choice of:

'Community buses' – which involves picking up the elderly for hospital appointments, taking them shopping, these are run by the council, wasn't sure I would be suited to this.

I could work in a charity shop!! And of course, I choose the charity shop.

He lets me go home that afternoon, and I get my new assignment details through the post.

I arrive at the British Heart Foundation shop in Nantwich. Working every Saturday and one day in the week – this is great. I learn how to dress the window attracting more customers, interact with the shoppers boosting takings as they buy more. I bring my daughter with me on Saturdays she prices the items and steams the clothes upstairs. I develop a great relationship with the manager. I am even asked if I would consider a manager position with the company.

She is a single lady I suggest she joins the dating agency, she comes to my house on her day off and fills in her profile, I don't charge her a joining for fee. I cannot tell you if she was successful, as I did not check up on how she was doing.

One afternoon I'm sat with Chris. He has created an online shopping portal similar to Amazon, one of the first ever in the UK. I was working on this and successfully bringing in contracts from High Street stores.

Chris decides he wants to open an office in the USA and asked me to go there?

Fuck! Can you believe it? Boston is the chosen city. One minute I'm going to prison, and the next one I'm going to Boston. Of course I accepted. I still need to finish my community service. I ended up working full time in the shop for about two weeks, making sure I complete one hundred and forty hours. I must say working there was a great experience.

Before going to Boston, Chris bought a seventy foot yacht which was berthed in Poole, Dorset. He invites a few people to join him on its maiden voyage, and I travel in the brand new Bentley with one of my dear friends and colleagues, Lulu.

We arrive at the harbour late that afternoon. The owner is telling us not to sail as the sea is rough and the Bay of Biscay is very unsettled, however Chris insists on going. We've been shopping and bought all these supplies which are loaded onto the yacht. It is amazing, with four bedrooms, large living space and kitchen.

We set sail that evening not too far into the journey I'm sick. The sea is rough, it's grey, it's raining and I'm rolling around in the bathroom, just being sick the whole time. There's another chap, head of marketing – sick, the MD of the dating agency is sick, just Lulu and Chris are ok. This is a nightmare there's nowhere to go we're all sick. Chris is the captain. He just carries on, tells us we are soft. I think it took two days or even longer to get to France. I did not stop being sick the whole journey.

By the time we docked, I was white as a ghost and extremely dehydrated, along with my colleagues. The first thing I do is look for a flight home. I'm really devastated that I cannot stay on the yacht, where it was heading for Spain then Portugal. I flew home the next day and stayed in the hotel that night back on dry land.

I rest awhile and I go back to work, I am preparing my youngest daughter for our move to Boston. Once Chris got back we organised the trip. Lulu is coming with us and Tom who is an ex-army captain. I think Chris just liked him as I am not sure what he did in the company. Lulu was Chris' PA and spoke three languages. She went to Oxford. I found a lovely apartment for Victoria and myself, arrange a meeting with the school in Boston. The day comes for us to fly out. We start a new adventure.

Audrey

You Think It's Easy Money But It's Not Carmen

How I met Audrey: broke, needed a job, MEN paper, jobs section, no qualifications desperate times, mouths to feed, bills to pay. What's this I see, receptionist? Great. A short walk from home. Ladies' evening in a health club. Ha Ha. Sauna. Call them up, get an interview. So, get a little dressed up, look ok. A small yellow building, you go up a flight of stairs straight from the street. The door at the top of the stairs, opens onto a reception area, small but clean, bright, the office is off the reception, out comes this little woman called Cathy she is the boss' PA. Asks me to come into the office and meet Mr Smith. He owns the building, which has a builder's yard downstairs and the health club upstairs. I'll take you on a tour after I've described Mr Smith and Cathy. Cathy first: about 5ft tall, mousey brown hair in a bob with a curl, early thirties, a plain Jane, she always wore cardigan and jumpers with a flared skirt and flat shoes. A little chubby. I was to find out she was the boss. To get to Mr Smith you had to go to her first. I think she was in love with Mr Smith. Mr Smith was in his fifties, overweight, wore an ill-fitting toupee, about 5ft 7in in height, he always wore shirt and trousers which his belly hung over. Cathy ran the show. The interview went well. I would do three days a week maybe more if they needed me. I would work the ladies' days, well the ladies' evenings. My hours would be ten till ten. Do the towels, make drinks, do the cleaning. See to the clients. Let me show you round the building. So we are at reception, behind reception is a small room where we kept the towels, toiletries, we had our lunch in there. The office was off the reception. As we come from behind the reception, you walk down a small hallway which had small cubicles off it. Enough room for a massage couch, chair, small cabinet, hook for clothes. They didn't have doors; you pulled a red curtain across and he had a spy hole cut out in the wood frame. The dirty bastard. Ha Ha. One of the cubicles had a solarium in it, an old-fashioned sunbed. It looked like a grill, you lay down on the couch and the grill was above you. Another cubicle had a Slendertone machine in it, which a lot of the ladies used, it's an inch loss machine. Come back up the corridor turn right walk into the pool/snooker room. Then the locker room, off there the sauna, steam and cold plunge, all tiled, piped music. Whoever was on duty had to clean all those areas, do the towels, empty the bins, hoover and mop at the end of the shift. You put the towels to dry in the sauna, they came out like boards. We used to get paid about £2 an hour. It's time to meet Audrey. In her forties, tall, slim, curly tight perm with a fringe. I think she had false teeth; she had that type of mouth. Busty. Never wore a bra. She had great boobs. Her uniform was a t-shirt low scooped neckline, A-line skirt, belt and Scholl sandals (sexy or what). She was so nice once you got to know her. Now she was a busy lady, she wasn't too forth coming in telling why? But I picked up the gist of what she did. So, the guys paid to come in and use the facilities, book in for massage, well as smart as I thought I was, it was an eye opener. No sex in them days, first massage guided by the guy. Conversation went like. 'What's your name? How long have you worked here?'

Me, 'Not long.'

'What do you do?'

'What do you mean? Hand job? Tit roll? Oral? Oral and tit job? 'What do you normally have? OK. With a condom?'

'Audrey does it without.'

220

No wonder she is so busy. Sometimes we worked on our own or there was two of us on together. I soon caught on to how Audrey worked. Hence the t-shirt pulled down and her blow jobs. I thought because I was younger, slimmer, pert boobs that I would be busier. Doesn't work like that. Experience is what the guys want. You learn to tune into the game, be sexy without giving too much away, nice sexy underwear, smell gorgeous, talk dirty. Downside; smelly men. Fat bellies. Grabbing hands always trying to get more than what they were paying for. I had a good run there for about a year and half. Even Mr Smith said, 'Can you pop into the Slendertone room?' He's sat with his bits out asking for a hand job, always paid, copped a feel now and then. I became as popular as Audrey. She was a nice ordinary lady, had her man, went to the pub Friday and Saturday nights. Funny thing is I enjoyed working there. Especially on the ladies' evenings, we would have some great laughs. I remember one of the girls going under the solarium, I can't remember for how long. When she came in the next week, she had a handprint on her tummy. It was white where a hand had been. We also had a receptionist that worked the ladies' evenings, she was so posh, always on a diet, drove an MG sports car. She and I became good friends in work. She always wore expensive jewellery, nice clothes. A few of the guys that came in were on the town scene, knew the Quality St, some of the club owners. When I went to the Press Club later in life I was to bump into some of them. When I was there, I did my house up, I think Mr Smith and Cathy had an affair. She had a child. Maybe it was his? He was married with grown up sons.

- 'Thanks for the break.' The famous words.
- You think it's easy money but it's not.
- Why? Could you do it?
- A stranger putting their hands on you.
- You pretending it's great.
- The danger of them switching.
- The police.

- A sigh and a prayer.
- Liking the money.
- Good while it lasted.
- Straight job next time.

Dysfunctional Families

Catherine

I start this today with a heavy heart as I listen to my dear friend tell our group she is an alcoholic.

The story she told was one of sadness, self-blame, hate, feeling that everyone will be ashamed of her, when we listen to her story of an abusive, drunk, violent father – full of misery.

I start to remember my own pain, my childhood, being brought up in this loveless home. I try to remember a time when my mum told me she loved me or praised me for something I had achieved or simply thanked me for something I had done.

I only remember one occasion and I think I was four, I had chicken pox, my vest is stuck to my body. Mum has to dab every spot away from my vest, and my vest away from my skin. She did it with gentleness and kindness being careful not to hurt me anymore than I was hurting. I remember she put me in the bath and bathed me. She wrapped me in a towel and hugged me, and I remember that feeling so well. I don't recall ever having it again.

I cannot remember a time when mum said she loved me, or any of my siblings, as young kids we always fought with each other, we never got along, always surviving on the edge of life.

I once remember mum going out, my youngest sister was less than one year old, which made me round about five and my eldest sister six. We were left in charge of the baby and given a small jar of what we thought were baby sweets.

'If she cries just give her one of these.' Mum went and left us alone.

Of course, the baby cried as babies do. Each time we couldn't stop her crying we gave her one of the baby sweets. We put her in the middle of a double bed and were jumping up and down just like a trampoline around her and when she cried we gave her another baby sweet.

By the time mum got home she had gone to sleep. We showed mum what we had given her, and mum panicked, she is shouting at us screaming, 'Why did we do that?' Telling us we were naughty.

She was in a rage, aggressive, frightened, she runs out of the house with the baby. We lived opposite St Mary's Hospital at the time. Turns out they were not baby sweets; they were junior aspirin. We were blamed for a crisis that could have ended up in a death.

How does a mum go out and leave her children home alone? She would often go out and not come back, sometimes the whole weekend. She left us when she went to work in the pub and came home late at night.

One night we were bathing my baby brother Douglas, we put him in the baby bath on the kitchen floor, the water was cold so we warmed it up with boiling water from the kettle, we put the three-month-old baby in the bath and the water was still cold so I poured boiling water from the kettle into the bath whilst my brother was still in there. Boiling water splashed him, I had no idea why he was screaming, so I quickly washed him, and I got him out. He kept crying, I dried him, he was still crying, I lay on the sofa with him, gave him a kit-kat to help him stop crying. He fell asleep, kit-kat still in his mouth, exhausted from the crying and the pain no doubt.

I moved from the sofa and he wakes up crying again. I pick him up and I see a huge blister the size of my fist on his back. He was burnt from the boiling water. I'm crying now, scared mum will go mad, she arrives home, we show her the burn, and I remember her screaming and swearing, 'Fucking idiots.' She puts cream on his burn. She did not take him to the hospital. It was a serious burn, but the next day she went to work as usual and left us alone.

If a mum did that today would she lose her children? Did mum care? I don't think she did we were just a burden to her – five children, all different dads, we were brought up seeing men in and out of the house, men who would beat her.

One man would lie in bed in the morning, my elder sister and I would see his willy, he would tell us to pull it until the white stuff came out, what the fuck! He would tell us to put matchsticks inside his urethra. We did. We didn't know any better: we were eight and nine years old. I told my mum what happened. She was in the kitchen cooking sausages. She slapped my face, told me not to be so stupid. He lay upstairs in the bed. He once ripped her dress off her back, in front of our eyes. Mum drank and smoked a lot in those days.

Sometimes we would come down the stairs in the morning, the fire still lit, Irish music playing, the house was warm but I knew it was wrong. There was a man – the husband of her friend – he would stay over. I remember he would ask my sister to sit on his knee. She was in her nighty. He never asked me. I wouldn't go near him. He would sing Irish songs to her and tell stories. I never trusted him.

We had a lodger. He was a lorry driver so went away for weeks at a time. When he came back a lady used to come to the house. Her name was Beryl. She wore short skirts and high shoes, lots of make-up, she had long black hair, she would go into his room. When she came out she would say thanks to mum. I remember sometimes she left money on the sideboard. When he was away, we would play in his room and find used condoms on the floor, not sure why we were in there. Just being kids I suppose.

My life was full of uncertainty, full of fear of the unknown, full of disappointment. I've learned to expect nothing, with low self-esteem, no confidence. I wore glasses at the age of five was known as speccy four eyes, and later Joe 90. I came to accept that this was the norm and I was worthless. I would tell my mum. She didn't care, my siblings didn't care, none of us cared. We were all too busy scratching through life, seeing the violence, the men and the drinking.

As I grew up I started running away from home. I never remember loving mum or my family, except my brother Douglas. I would hang out on the street drinking cider mess around with boys thinking that they might like me, they didn't. They would call me names. By the time I was fifteen and I put my own self into care, I was hanging around the streets of Moss Side, going to the Reno till four in the morning, staying at different peoples' houses, no direction and no one cared. I didn't care.

I listen to my friend today and I understand why she, we, drank. I used to drink sometimes a bottle of gin or vodka or whatever came my way. I thought I was having fun. I wasn't. I was fighting the pain of my neglect, from my soulless mother, my dysfunctional home. I look and listen to my generation – Irish Catholic, tormented by the nuns, by the people who were supposed to care for us. I understand why we had troubled teenage years, why we readily accepted violence, and abuse in our own adult lives. It was learned behaviour. A conditioning from our parents. Their cold unforgiving eyes, the ruthlessness in their beatings.

My mum once stood on my face with her high heel shoe. She hit me with the poker. My brother had to pull her off me. She smashed my head on the front door. She would beat me with the sweeping brush, her bare hands, once she threw milk bottles at me, she had no control over her emotions, her temper, her rages, she must have been ill. Nowadays you can get help for this. She still has no remorse she lives in denial of everything. My siblings allow her to do so, but I don't.

I rarely see her; she sometimes leaves unpleasant messages on my phone.

I am mad with her today, and mad with every parent who behaved like her.

'LOOK what you have done!'

'Look at the hurt and the pain you caused!'

'Look at my friend, an alcoholic, a kind wonderful lady, a victim of her childhood, and now she feels shame.'

What does love feel like? If you are not shown love, how do you know what it feels like?

For most of my life I thought I was commitment phobic as I have never fully committed myself to anyone. I realise now that that is because I never allowed myself to be with someone I might like too much, the fear of rejection and hurt did not afford me the luxury of this.

Instead I chose men who were older than me, abused me, I learned to use them for my personal needs, and pretended I loved them to keep the peace when most of the time they disgusted me.

Disgusted me because of the age difference, because of their bullying, their controlling behaviour, that I stupidly accepted thinking I might grow to love them. Or maybe I was convinced by them that no one would ever really love me, and to be fair why would they I had nothing to offer. Since my childhood years I was a misfit, I hung out on the street had a black baby, that made me white trash! This feeling stayed with me far too long.

Then one day I realised I wasn't a commitment phobic. When my children were born I gave them love, commitment, shared all their happiness, achievements, pain and glory. It is now I realise I just never found the person who accepted me unconditionally as I accepted my children, and in return they accept me.

I think I have learned how to love and how to give love. I remember when we became young adults, my sister Anne and brother Douglas, we learned to hold each other and not to be scared to show our feelings. This was nice. Mum still cannot do that with me, nor me with her. I think I hold the most pain from those early years. And I don't hide how I feel these days.

I could have been my friend today standing there telling the story of being an alcoholic, but I escape that. In my later adult life, I have seen love, from my friend that I didn't think I was worthy of. My dearest friend Jasmin, so posh, so eloquent, so charming, so kind. We met whilst working at the dating agency. Everyone loved her. We always chatted. She could see the bullying from the American lady.

Jasmine taught me how to be proud of myself. She picked me up when I was down, she stood by my side when I nearly went to prison, she judges no one, accepts life and taught me how to love myself, which I unashamedly do now. I will always be grateful to her for that.

I believe my mum, my friend's dad, the catholic religion, have a lot to answer for.

I have tried not to make the same mistakes as they have, but none of us are perfect.

I hope children don't suffer in silence as I did for many decades.

My friend K, I salute you.

Kloisters

The Tax Man
Carmen

Kloisters nightclub – great night out for a lot of people, Bill Kerfoot owned it, plus Jilly's and Genèvieve's. I started working there as a barmaid on the top bar. It was on Oxford Rd, City Centre. I loved working there. Joe the manager, we will call the doormen Pete, Chubby and John. You came in off Oxford Rd, down the stairs into a small foyer, where you paid fifty pence in before a certain time (ladies only), £1.00 for the guys. £2.00 Friday/Saturday nights. Go through the doors into the nightclub. Through the door to the right, down the corridor to Joe's office. Stand straight and look ahead there was the club's big dance floor – pillars from ceiling to floor that looked like soldiers. If you turned left there was a bar run by a girl called Rebecca (she was Jewish), she wore a Shakel (wig), she was a right fiddle, thought she was the boss. You had the top bar which was my bar, Ha Ha, a lot of the time. Then there was the long bar on the dance floor. The kitchen was off the dance floor. As you go back towards going out up the stairs, to the left was a very small bar, where Joe used to watch the club and get his drinks. The décor was lots of wood, the DJ box was to the right of the dance floor slightly raised. I worked the top and long bar. Thursday, Friday and Saturday nights were packed to the ceiling. The drinks were about fifty pence a shot (starting price). I did have a nice little earner going in the club. Saturday nights were the best, as it so busy. I used to slip my fiddle into my tip jar, as we kept our tips, no sharing. When my family or friends came in, they rarely paid for a full round. Especially when I was on the top bar. That was the spot right up the corner. We had two tills on that bar, we each had our till. I became friends with Joe's wife. We had nights out, she came to the club a lot. Probably to keep an eye on Joe, with all the totty that was around. I also started cleaning in the club, then on the door as well taking the ticket money. The door men had a little fiddle going with the woman who was taking the ticket money, so I got on that with them too. In the school holidays when the kids were off, I would take them with me to the club when I was cleaning. They loved it. I worked with an Italian woman. She would open the kitchen, and cook the kids' lunches, she was very funny. Burger and chips. They would look for money round the club, we played music while we worked. I remember it was *War of the Worlds*. It was the big soundtrack back then. Cleaning the club was an eye opener, there was a lot of stealing in the club, handbags found in the toilets, cleaning up sick, finding underwear, cleaning up after fights. Remember Rebecca who worked the small bar, well one shift I went to work with her, she did things different, when she went off the bar, she said I had to put all the coppers that I got into a pot and let her know how it was, I don't know how or what she did, but that was her fiddle. She disliked anyone on her bar apart from one girl who mainly worked her bar, she may have been in on it with her. My tips from Saturday night, were my Reno money. The Quality St guys used to call in to have a drink with Joe. They were friends of Kerfoot, they were the originals. I heard a few years after I left that Joe had a heart attack and died. It was the booze, cigs and club life I bet.

The Tax Man. Well I have to go back to working for Bridie and Trevor (names changed). Here and in Blackpool. I worked Manchester for a while then they asked me to go to Blackpool. They were good bosses, looked out for and after the girls, wanted their girls to have health checks, eat well. Bridie worked also at Blackpool with the girls. Blackpool was very busy as you can imagine. Visitors, Party Political Conferences. Yeah well this is how I met the Tax Man. It was about 1979/1981. When I was in Blackpool, we were very professional in how we dressed; we wore blue beauty dresses with our professional badges. Underneath was the sexy underwear, suspenders, stockings and the heels. Our rooms were on the ground floor of a massive Victorian building. We had certificates for massage. That somehow made what we did legal. We were making money – when we worked on Saturdays and didn't have a lift home, we would get a cab back to Manchester. We felt we were getting watched and followed home. We went quiet. Then we got raided. I was in that day, got taken to the police station, kept in overnight. It was bloody awful. There was three of us working that day, one of the girls sang like a canary. The police took the dom equipment, rubbish, anything they could find. Anyway down the line we go to court twice. And final hearing, Bridie and Trevor get sentenced. And two of us get done for aiding and abetting in the management of a brothel. We are in the MEN. Fast forward to 1983, I get a letter from the Tax Office. They want to see me. Off I go, not knowing what I'm walking into. Me heavily pregnant. Get shown into a little office and there he is, this little insignificant man, 'Sit down please.' He starts by asking me lots of questions. He lifts some papers on his desk and I recognize the handwriting on this small piece of paper, on it are the days and cash that I had written down. There were about four weeks' takings written down. He worked it out that if I had worked for Bridie and Trevor for a certain time, I owed a lot of money in taxes. I got a solicitor to speak for me. In the end I had to pay a lot of money to the Tax Office, over a long period of time. I had to prove that I had not worked for Bridie and Trevor for as long as he thought I had. Which I did. The police gave the Tax Man the paper. Because I proved that I had a job and paid taxes and didn't work for them as long as he thought, it wasn't as bad as it could have been. I stored jewellery and fur coats away as I was told the bailiffs could come and take things out of my home, they weren't coming.

The Tax Man's last words to me were, 'Let's not meet again.'

xxx

Deepest Darkest Secret

Catherine

April 1974, I'm leaving Darley House the care home I have come to love, having lived there for two years. I feel sad that it's time to go leaving my friend Christine and the other girls behind, the Nuns wish me good luck and say goodbye. I am taken to a foster home in Gorton, my care worker Mrs Keesh takes me there. We drove in silence. When we arrived my first thought is that the house doesn't smell very clean, maybe there were cats? I'm not a fan. I cannot remember the lady or her name, she takes me to my room, it wasn't pleasant not like Darley House. She has at least one maybe two children of her own. They were young under the age of seven, maybe they were foster children. The girl comes into my room, she stares at me, I ignore her and finally she leaves. I am sad, feeling alone, lost, hurting inside. I go to the bathroom there is a shower over the bath with a blue plastic shower curtain the type that sticks to you when you are in the shower. Around the bath was black 'mould' I suppose! It was just wear and tear of a home and I hated it.

I would get up every morning get ready for work in my room, and leave the house for the day, often not returning until late at night. I never told anyone in work where I had moved to. I did not go back for dinner and would often go to the pub with my friends or meet Christine when she could come into town.

We had been planning a trip to Lourdes at Darley House before I left and everyone was very excited by it, but I was no longer to be part of that. This made me very sad and lonely.

I never spoke to anyone in the foster house and I told the lady not to cook for me. Working in Manchester as an account holder for a freight company and covering reception which I loved, gave me my own money to feed myself.

One of the girls I worked with had befriended me. She took me to her house it was beautiful. Her mum was a seamstress, she made me a pair of dusty pink trouser, she had made them bigger than I wanted so she put extra buttons in the waist band so I could adjust them.

Things weren't going well at the foster home. The lady has told me I need to find somewhere else as I don't seem to be happy there. My social worker takes me to my mum's who had agreed have me.

'Here we go again,' I think to myself, but it has to be done. I carry on working in Manchester and on Sunday I work at the golf club washing pans. Things are ok at mum's; I work, pay rent and I can see my brother all the time. My eldest sister has gone to Guernsey to work for the summer holiday season, we often wrote to each other. That's strange as we were not close, well, to be fair we didn't know how to be. She was very happy there and made lots of new friends and a boyfriend. Yes!!! A real boyfriend.

'And so, I'll start to reveal the secret for the first time in my life.'

I'm just getting on with life. One morning I go to my mum's bedroom and tell her I am in pain, and that I had been in pain all night, walking up and down the room. Mum jumps out of bed. 'Feckin' hell,' she shouts, 'This is it.' ?? I look at her but I'm in too much pain. Mum went next door asked the neighbour to help with the kids, there were three of them two brothers and my younger sister. She also called a taxi. It was September and the sun was shining as we got into the taxi. I was just in a daze. 'Hurry up,' mum kept saying to the taxi driver, it was rush hour and we were going to Withington hospital. I could see mum's face white and strained, she put her hand on my leg and said we will be there soon. I didn't respond. We arrive at the hospital everything is a blur I can hear nurses calling and I'm on a bed. I can't see any faces.

So I woke up in a hospital bed in a room on my own, mum has gone home, I have no idea of the time or day, the sun was shining though. A nurse came in she asked me how I was feeling? I am groggy, and I feel pain but I'm not sure why I am there. 'What happened?' I ask the nurse. She leaves the room and another nurse appears. She tells me she is 'sorry' the baby did not survive. 'What do you mean?' I ask. I am confused. Had the baby been born? I was not aware. She told me when I came to the hospital it was time for the baby to be born, but too late to save the baby's life. ?? I was numb and in shock, I suppose I didn't know what to say. She told me the baby was a girl and asked if I would like to give her a name. I called her Samantha. The nurse said she was sorry for me, I told her I was going to have the baby adopted. There were no tears just shock. The nurse said oh well maybe it was for the best then. ??? WTF!! WTF!!!! Who would say that. I had just been through the biggest trauma of my young life. And I've just been told it was probably for the best.

I remember asking later that day, where the baby was, and will there be a funeral, I cannot get this exactly right did I dream it? Or make up the response?

I was told as the baby did not breathe there would be no funeral, no burial, I don't know if the next part is correct, but it's what I remember. She told me that the body would be incinerated!!!!! I didn't understand! Would someone do that?

I never checked out what happened, I almost felt like I had no right to. I know I asked the midwife who visited me about a death certificate. 'Oh you don't want to worry yourself about that.' I know mum felt the same way, I was just told to forget it, it is over now.

I don't believe there was a death certificate. So she was never really given a name.

You see this was the reason I had to leave Darley House. I never visited a doctor or went to an antenatal class, no one from social services came to see me, after I left the hospital. No one ever spoke about my incident, 'My Trauma' !!!! it was never discussed again. There was no one to help me, with my grief, my trauma, no one to talk to.

Instead like a tumbleweed I was allowed to roam, to carry on as if nothing had happened, nothing changing in my body, my young life. My friend's mum knew. That's why she put the extra buttons on the trousers, she never said a word. She used to cook nice food and sometimes she would stroke my head.

Once I was back at mum's after the ordeal that no one spoke about, the midwife visited me, I was in a huge amount of pain and later found out that I had a tilted womb which had not gone back into place, I don't know how they fixed it. My boobs were massive and like rocks. The midwife told me to take Epsom salts, pick myself up and be glad I can start over again. Another WTF!!!!!! moment.

All this time mum is around we never talk about what happened to me. She has my three siblings to care for plus I am sure she would have been working.

Eventually I get better, and start working again, I am really slim so no one ever knew what had happened to me. I never cried; I just froze this memory in the pit of my stomach so deep I didn't think it would rise up again.

My sister is back from Guernsey, she has lost her boyfriend to her best friend. (Yikes!!) She gets a job in the local cinema and carries on as usual, no one talking about her ordeal either.

I just drank a lot all of the time, I just went out after work drank and listened to my Marvin Gaye *What's Going On* album in the deepest darkest hole I had ever been in, drifting, hardened to anything that touched me, like a mechanical robot going on with my day to day life, always a mess, moving from one bad situation to another I was sixteen/seventeen years old.

Forty-two years years later I'm at the cemetery burying my brother, I came across a headstone that simply said:-

'She was born asleep'

This made me cry, and cry and I'm crying now. For the first time I cried for you Samantha. I suddenly understood you were born asleep. She had no one, a tiny baby who was not allowed to breath, to look and see her mum's face. Who knows what the outcome would have been if she had been given that opportunity to take a breath. I used to visit the grave often and still do when I am at the cemetery. I would say a prayer for you Samantha, for the first time I acknowledge your existence, I regret I didn't see you, I have no idea what your face was like, but I am sure it was beautiful. I couldn't count your fingers, your toes or smile with you. I hope the angels have taken good care of you. For the first time I say RIP my baby, who was born asleep.

I have to stop writing now, as I remember those days, the times when no-one cared, or knew how to care. But no one offered me anything, I was just told to get on with it. Get on with something so mammoth, something that until now I have never spoken about.

So, the only people who knew about this, was my eldest sister, mum and Christine, apart from the social services who did nothing for me, they did not introduce me to an adoption agency, no one told me about antenatal, or visiting my doctor if I even had one. I just ignored what was happening, and so did everyone else. Is it any wonder I was able to live two lives always hiding from the truth, the reality.

I never had a role model, someone to show me right from wrong, someone I could trust, someone who I felt safe with. Someone who looked out for me who made me feel loved and not worthless. I literally was left to roll around just like a tumbleweed, gathering more and more weeds, until one day

I found my own strength. This took many years and more traumas than I care to mention.

I know mum did her best to care for me after the event, but how could she, when she really could not care for herself. I thank her for what she did, and for taking me to the hospital. I am sure this was traumatic for her.

I am sorry to my girls for never telling you.

I have always believed this was something to be ashamed of, to hide away, never admit to. When in reality, I was just another victim of circumstance.

Unable to cry for forty-two years years! About one of the most traumatic happenings in my life. Well I have cried now.

My sister asked me recently if I had any traumas in my life.

I didn't reply.